UK IN Eurovision

The highs and lows

Andy Bishop

UK IN Eurovision

The highs and lows

Andy Bishop

WYMER
PUBLISHING
Bedford, England

First published in 2023 by Wymer Publishing
Bedford, England www.wymerpublishing.co.uk Tel: 01234 326691
Wymer Publishing is a trading name of Wymer (UK) Ltd

Copyright © 2023 Andy Bishop / Wymer Publishing.

Print edition (fully illustrated): **ISBN: 978-1-915246-26-4**

Edited by Jerry Bloom.

The Author hereby asserts his rights to be identified
as the author of this work in accordance with sections
77 to 78 of the Copyright, Designs & Patents Act 1988.

All rights reserved. No part of this publication may be
reproduced or transmitted in any form or by any means,
electronic or mechanical, including photocopying, or any
information storage and retrieval system, without written
permission from the publisher.

This publication is sold subject to the condition that it shall not,
by way of trade or otherwise, be lent, re-sold, hired out or
otherwise circulated without the publishers' prior consent in any
form of binding or cover other than that in which it is published
and without a similar condition including this condition
being imposed on the subsequent purchaser.

eBook formatting by Coinlea.
Printed and bound in Great Britain by
CMP, Dorset.

A catalogue record for this book is available from the British Library.

Typeset/Design by Andy Bishop / 1016 Sarpsborg
Cover design by 1016 Sarpsborg.

Contents

Introduction	7
The Early Years 1956-1969	9
The 1970s	37
The 1980s	63
The 1990s	83
The 2000s	109
The 2010s and onwards	129
The UK entrants at a glance	161
Results Scoreboards	163
References	194
Acknowledgements	194

Introduction

Eurovision... ask anybody what Eurovision means to them and you will get a divided answer, some hate it, and others love it. I am in the category of those that love it. It first came to my attention in 1974 when it was staged in Brighton and of course the winners were ABBA. It blew my mind, I hadn't seen anything like it, ABBA were of course amazing, but to me the most interesting aspect of the event was the scoring, I was transfixed, and have been ever since.

Some people say it's politically driven, friendly neighbours voting for each other. For example the Scandinavian countries usually stick together, that seems to infuriate the journalists. I find it all part of the fun. A few years ago the media in the UK was blaming Brexit for our bad results, but that is not entirely true, if you have a good song the audience will vote for it, unfortunately over the years we have had some woeful entries that got what they deserved.

Also Eurovision has changed significantly over the years, from only eight countries battling it out in 1956 to over forty countries in 2022. There are thirty-seven countries taking part this year in 2023. Eurovision is now the biggest global music competition in the world today, with over 161 million viewers in 2022. In 2023 there will be over thirty-seven public broadcasters screening the event. It is a competition on a massive scale, you won't find anything like it. In 2015 the contest in Vienna was bigger than the Superbowl with viewing figures in excess of 200 million.

There have been rule changes and voting changes continuously throughout the years. I haven't dwelled on these, I have just mentioned any changes if I think it was necessary. It is also the same with the countries taking part. Initially Eurovision was just held over one day, now it is a complete week, two semi-finals and a final, with the host nation organising a whole week of events and festivities.

If you look back over the years, Eurovision has had some megastars taking part from Celine Dion to Julio Iglesias, but this book is solely about the United Kingdom entries with a few facts thrown in about each year. If you want an in-depth book on everything Eurovision there a lots of other books out there, this is a simply a reference of where, when and who represented the UK, and of course where they ended up, high or low, all in one book.

The UK have had some very diverse artists representing them over the years — those that were already stars and those that have gone on to be superstars at home and internationally. There have also been those that have been shockingly awful and have disappeared shortly afterwards. That to me is one of the reasons the Eurovision is so diverse. In some ways it is a relief that the UK doesn't have to qualify for the final. I believe for many years we would not have made it through the semi-final.

The book is split up into decades to make it easier. Whilst compiling this I have had a bit of fun at the same time by scoring each competing artist out of six, and where an entry has won that actual year I have placed a party popper. Where they have come last there is a rubbish bin.

Don't take my comments or scoring too seriously. I am not a professional music journalist. I appreciate all music and anybody who performs in front of an audience I admire, however bad they are.

I have included newspaper clippings of the time and some pictures to compliment the text.

One outcome that I haven't been able to complete is the result of this years competition, as the book has gone to print before the final. I wish all the luck to Mai Muller in Liverpool, I'm sure she is as excited by representing the UK as us fans are watching it.

Long may Eurovision continue!

My scoring dice   Winning year   Artist last place

The Early Years 1956-1969

1956

1956 was the first ever Eurovision song contest. It was held in Lugano, Switzerland. Other than the host nation, six other countries contested the competition: The Netherlands, Belgium, Italy, France, Germany and Luxembourg, with each country performing two songs, Switzerland coming out winners with song titled *Refrain* performed by Lys Assia.

It was mainly a radio broadcast but there were a few cameras filming enabling those lucky enough with TV sets to watch.

The United Kingdom declined to take part due to the fact it was organising it's own domestic song writing competition.

The Early Years

1957

Patricia Bredin

1957 was the second Eurovision Song Contest and was held on Sunday, 3rd March hosted in Frankfurt, West Germany.

Ten countries took part with the United Kingdom, Austria and Denmark participating for the first time. Each country could award one vote to their favourite song and the voting was now done in public to allow the viewers and listeners at home to follow along with the voting.

The winner of the contest was the Netherlands, with a song titled *Net als toen* performed by Corry Brokken, who also represented the Netherlands the year before.

Britain was represented by Patricia Bredin with a song titled *All*, written by Reynell Wreford and Alan Stranks.

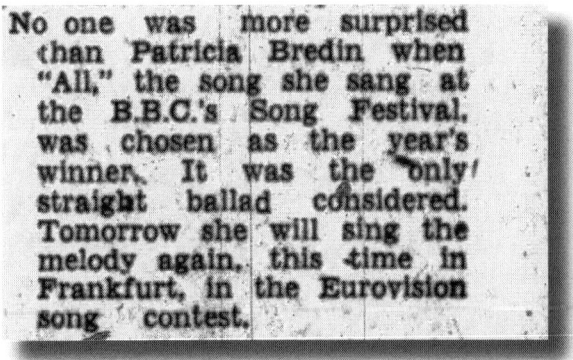

A newspaper clipping from the Birmingham Mail, 2nd March, 1957.

The song was chosen by the BBC after coming through three semi-finals and a final with regional juries allocating scores.

Breden is an English actress and one-time singer, she has become best know for being the first person to represent the UK at Eurovision, also her song *All* is the first song to be sung in English at Eurovision.

Accompanied by an orchestra, it was a typical ballad sung with a very nice mezzo soprano voice from a by-gone era.

She came seventh in the final with six points.

One fact about *All* is that up until 2015 it was the shortest performance in the history of the contest with a time of one minute, fifty-two seconds, only to be beaten by Finland's Pertti Kurikan Nimipäivät with a song titled *Aina mun pitää* which was one minute twenty-seven seconds long.

After Eurovision Patricia continued her career in musicals, film and TV variety shows, for three months in 1962 she succeeded Julie Andrews in the Broadway production of Camelot.

Author's Comment:
I am not a music critic I only write what I think, negative or positive about the song/artist and performance.

Having not been around at the time when this competition took place I can only judge retrospectively and the song fitted in with the music at that time. It could easily have been a film score from the 1950s, and Bredin's performance was entertaining.

The Early Years

Patricia Bredin the first artist to represent the UK at Eurovision.

1958

The third Eurovision song contest took place on 12th March in Hilversum, the Netherlands. This was the first time the contest was hosted by the winning country from the previous year. Which has been the case ever since, but there have been a few exceptions.

This wasn't going to be the original venue, the UK was going to host the contest. However, due to the UK failing to get an agreement with various artistic unions the BBC withdrew their bid to participate and stage the contest.

Ten countries took part with Sweden taking the UK's place. The winner of the contest was France with the song *Dors, mon amour* performed by André Claveau.

The Early Years

1959

Pearl Lavinia Carr and Edward Victor Johnson

The contest was held in France at the Palais des Festivals eet des Congres in Cannes on 11th March.

A total of eleven countries took part with the UK represented by Pearl Lavinia Carr and Edward Victor Johnson, husband and wife entertainers who were popular during the 1950s and early 1960s.

The song was *Sing Little Birdie*, a catchy little duet which was chosen from twelve other songs by different artists after two semi-finals and then a final, scored by regional juries.

At the Eurovision Final the song came in second place with sixteen points. The Netherlands were the outright winners with a song *Een Beetje* performed by Teddy Scholten.

This was the start of many second-place finishes for the UK.

Finals in the Eurovision Song Contest in Cannes

Coventry Evening Telegraph 11th March 1959.

By MONITOR

TONIGHT is Eurovision song contest night. At 8.0 the B.B.C. will relay from the Palais des Festivals, Cannes, a ⸺-minute programme during which the 1959 winner will be chosen. There will be 12 juries, consisting of ten people, in each of the competing countries. They will record votes for every tune except the one entered by their own country.

The British entry — the best of a rather bad lot — is "Sing Little Birdie," which will be sung by Pearl Carr and Teddy Johnson.

Author's Comment:
Super catchy tune, entertaining performance, but it is even clear from this early era that the media was already picking fault with Eurovision, (last paragraph on newspaper clipping).

1960

Bryan Johnson

This was one of those exceptions where the previous wining country didn't host the competition.

The UK staged the contest in London at the Royal Festival Hall on March 29th.

Although the Netherlands won the contest in 1959 they declined to host the competition due to the fact that they had staged the contest in 1958 and didn't want to do it twice in three years. So the contest organisers passed the baton to the second placed country, which was the UK. Thirteen countries entered this year.

As in all the preceding years, each country was represented by one song performed by up to two people on stage.

The voting was by Jury with each country consisting of ten members, who each gave one vote to their favourite song.

This year also allowed the juries to listen to a pre-recorded rehearsal of each song ahead of the live contest.

The contest was won by the French artist Jacqueline Boyer with a song titled *Tom Pillibi*.

The UK was represented by Bryan Johnson, with a song titled *Looking High, High, High*. Bryan was a singer and actor. He had tried to represent the UK in 1957, but had been eliminated in the semi-finals.

Looking High, High, High came in second place, with twenty-five points, the second year in a row the UK had just missed out.

The song did however give Bryan more success when it reached number twenty in the UK singles chart in April 1960.

Author's Comment:
Another catchy tune, would not be out of place in a 1960s cabaret club, just right for the era, well performed.

1961

The Allisons

On 18th March, France once again hosted the contest in the city of Cannes at Palais des Festivals et des Congrès, it was the first time the contest took place on a Saturday evening, which has continued up until this day. 1962 was the only exception to this.

Sixteen countries participated, three more than the previous year, the winner was Luxembourg with a song titled *Nous les amoureux* and sung by Jean-Claude Pascal.

The UK was represented by The Allisons with a song called *Are You Sure*.

The Allisons were a pop duo consisting of Bob Day and John Alford, they were marketed as brothers using the surname Allison.

Once again the UK was the bridesmaid and not the bride with a good second placing with twenty-four points.

Although the boys missed out on Euro glory they did go onto release the song on the Fontana records label where it made Number One in the *New Musical Express* pop chart, while in the Official Charts the song spent six weeks at number two and three weeks in the top four, selling over a million copies, thus earning a gold disc.

The duo disbanded in 1963, but they did make regular comebacks on the oldies circuit in the 1990s.

Author's Comment:
You can hear why this was a hit in the UK singles charts.
Two artists with super harmonic voices, well worth a listen if you haven't heard it.

The UK in Eurovision - *The Highs and Lows*

The Allisons

The Early Years

1962

Ronnie Carroll

Luxubourg hosted this year's Eurovision on Sunday, 18th March in Luxembourg City at the Villa Louvigny. This was the last time the contest was held on a Sunday.

Sixteen countries participated and once again France was the winner with the song *Un premier amour* performed by Isabelle Aubret.

The United Kingdom were represented by Ronnie Carroll a Northern Irish singer, entertainer. He won through the selection process with a song called *Ring-a-Ding-Girl*. He had tried to win through the selection process the year before.

In the Eurovision final the song came in fourth place with ten points.

Before and after Eurovision Carroll mainly played music halls and made guest appearances on TV shows and played cruise ships. He had a couple of top ten hits in 1962 and 1963.

In later life he went into politics and contested his home constituency Hampstead and Highgate in the 1997 general election.

Author's Comment:
A very good performance, strong voice, but I wonder why after The Allisons the year before the 'powers that be' chose a song again that wouldn't be out of place in a dance hall or cabaret club.

1963

Ronnie Carroll

France who won the previous year declined to host the event due to the fact they had hosted the event in 1959 and 1961, and it was proving to costly. Usually it's the second placed country that then hosts the contest, but on this occasion the UK and London stepped in again and the show was hosted at the BBC Television Centre on Saturday, 23rd March.

Sixteen countries participated and the winning country and song was Denmark with a song called *Dansevise* performed by Grethe & Jørgen Ingmann.

Before I go on to talk about the UK entry there was an interesting incident at this contest. When Norway announced their results, they made a mistake, the song number followed by the country should have been announced before awarding the points. They announced the points first, so they were asked to repeat the results in the correct order. Norway requested to repeat their results at the end, after all the other jury results had been read out.

When they did finally repeat their results they had mysteriously altered, this changed the outcome of the contest giving Denmark victory at the expense of Switzerland.

For the second time Ronnie Carroll was selected to represent the UK with a song titled *Say Wonderful Things,* written by Norman Newell and music by Philip Green. It came in fourth place same as the previous year but with a bigger points tally of twenty-eight.

Carroll still to this day remains the only singer to have represented the UK two years in succession, I believe this will never be broken.

Author's Comment:
Polished performance, but personally I found it non inspiring.

The Early Years

1964

Matt Monro

Denmark hosted this years event in Copenhagen at Tiviolis Koncertsal on Saturday, 21st March. Sixteen countries took part.

The winner was Italy with a song titled *Non ho l'eta* performed by Gigliola Cinquetti. She was the youngest winner of the contest yet, at the age of 16 years and 92 days, a record she held until 1986.

Another little fact about the song, it had one of the widest margins of victory ever in the competition, nearly three times as many points as the second-placed song.

During the contest, after the Swiss entry, a man holding a banner invaded the stage. This was hidden from the TV audience as they moved to a shot of the scoreboard whilst he was being removed.

The UK was represented by Matt Monro (real name Terence Parsons) who was chosen to sing six different songs in a selection process where juries made up of the public from sixteen different cities voted for their favourite. The winning song was titled *I Love The Little Things* written by Tony Hatch.

He performed at number eight in the final but once again the UK finished as the bridesmaid in second place with seventeen points, but it wasn't a close second place due the margin of the winning song.

All six songs were released on an extended play maxi single titled *A Song for Europe*, it reached number sixteen in the EP top twenty chart. The winning song was also released as a single but failed to make the UK charts.

Monro was one of the UK's great singers and was known to have a perfect baritone voice and went onto to have a very successful international career. He unfortunately died at a very young age of 54.

Author's Comment:
Great voice, nice song, interestingly there is actually no video of him performing at the contest.

The UK in Eurovision - *The Highs and Lows*

The Early Years

1965

Kathy Kirby

The contest moved on to Naples, Italy at the Sala di Concerto della RAI on 20th March. Eighteen countries participated which was a new record for entrants up until this point.

Luxembourg won the contest with a song sung by France Gall called *Poupée de cire, poupée de son*.

The United Kingdom held a national pre-selection to choose the song that would go to Europe this year. The BBC internally selected the singer again who performed six songs and the winning song was selected by viewers casting votes on postcards via post.

English singer Kathy Kirby, real name Catherine Ethel O'Rourke was the selected artist by the BBC. She had just achieved four top twenty hits and was one of the most recognised and best known personalities in British showbusiness and she had the looks of Marylin Monroe to go with it.

The winning song was *I Belong* written by singer Daniel Boone credited under his real name Peter Lee Stirling.

Unfortunately once again the song wasn't quite good enough and finished in second place, the fifth time a UK entry has finished second.

The six songs for Europe were released on an EP and reached number nine on the EP charts and the winning song was released as a single and reached number thirty-six in the singles chart.

Author's Comment:
This is one of those songs you need to hear a few times before you appreciate it, I am surprised it made second place, as I believe the juries wouldn't have heard the song that many times before scoring. Not one of my favourites.

The UK in Eurovision - *The Highs and Lows*

Liverpool Daily Post, Monday, March 22, 1965

I could have won, says Kathy

Kathy Kirby (right) congratulates Luxembourg's France Gall, the winner.

Kathy Kirby, edged into second place in Saturday's Eurovision song contest, was disappointed. She said she had been handicapped by being second in the programme. The winner, Luxembourg's France Gall, had the number 15 spot.

"If I'd been in the place of the Luxembourge girl, or near that spot, I'm sure I would have won," Kathy commented.

Mademoiselle Gall, who gave Luxembourg its first win in the contest since it began in 1956, bubbled over with delight. "I came down here expecting to get nothing but a plate of spaghetti," she exclaimed.

The British song—"I Belong," written by Peter Lee Stirling and Phil Peters—gained twenty-six points from juries in the eighteen countries taking part, six behind Luxembourg's winning entry, "Wax Doll, Straw Doll."

Irish singer is sixth

Third place was taken by France, whose singer was Guy Mardel, with twenty-two points. It was the sixth time in ten contests that Britain has been second. Fourth was Udd Jurgens (Austria) and fourteenth Bobby Solo (Italy). Butch Moore (Ireland) was sixth.

All competing countries voted to select the winner of the contest, which was televised in East and West Europe. Luxembourg, as the winner, will have the right to stage next year's contest. — Reuter and Associated Press.

I agreed with the jury...

A bird in the garden saluted the eve of official summertime outside my window. And, in my opinion, its song was infinitely better than any of those heard in the Eurovision song contest which the B.B.C. enabled us to see at Naples.

I am pleased to record, however, that when we came to No. 15, Luxembourg, I wrote down rather arrogantly, "This will be in the first three." The jury voted it No. 1 and I agreed with them.

Sung by a blonde Parisienne with eyes of startling vitality, the song had a novel theme and a tune that just escaped from the orthodox ruck.

Kathy's talent and faith

At these contests so much depends on the singers. This we saw in the United Kingdom's contribution, "I Belong," which Kathy Kirby, by a combination of talent and sheer faith, carried to second place, for reaching which we seem to have a natural gift.

But what an elaborate accouchement these Songs for Europe have. Almost worthy of the birth of a birth of a nation. Whatever the rest of the 150,000,000 views through (this was number quoted by David Jacobs) the most interesting part to me was the gradual accumulation of the votes. It reminded me of a General Election. N.G.P.

Liverpool Daily Post, March 22, 1965

The Early Years

1966

Kenneth McKeller

This years contest was held at the Villa Louvigny on 5th March in Luxembourg City in Luxembourg.

Eighteen countries took part and the winner this year was Austria with a song titled *Merci Chéri* performed and composed by Udo Jürgens. This was his third entry into the competition, third time lucky as they say.

Before we move onto the UK entry, a few things worth pointing out this year, firstly a new rule — a country could only sing in any of its native languages. I believe this was made due to the Swedish entry the previous year singing in English.

Also music experts were once again allowed to sit in the juries.

1966 also marked the first year a black person took part, Milly Scott representing the Netherlands.

This year also marked the arrival of the so called neighbourly or bloc voting which has seemingly plagued the contest up to present day.

Now onto the UK entry, usual format again, BBC picking a singer who performs the five shortlisted songs with the public voting for their favourite. Trained Opera singer and Scottish Tenor Kenneth McKeller was the chosen performer. The song that won this years selection was a ballad *A Man Without Love,* written by Peter Callender, music composed by Harry Rabinowitz.

McKeller performed in a kilt in the final, which apparently drew gasps from the audience. He came in a mid-table ninth place with eight points. The points came from only two countries and the Irish jury gave the UK top points, one of only two occasions the Irish have done so.

This was the worst result to date and he held this accolade until 1978.

Author's Comment:
One to forget I'm afraid!

The UK in Eurovision - *The Highs and Lows*

Sandie Shaw at the Eurovision Song Contest

The Early Years

1967

Sandie Shaw

Hofburg Palace, Vienna, Austria was the venue, with seventeen countries taking part, the absentee on this occasion was Denmark, who didn't take part again until 1978, the reason was the new director of entertainment thought the money could be better spent.

A specific note of interest this year is that this was the last black and white broadcast shown.

The UK entry Sandie Shaw, who was selected internally by the BBC, was chosen to sing five songs and as usual viewers chose the winning song, *Puppet on a String*, written by Bill Martin and Phil Coulter. (Not the same song Elvis Presley released)

Due to changing trends in the competition Sandie Shaw was the first real pop star to be chosen by the BBC to represent the UK.

This was a significant breakthrough for the UK, not only did *Puppet on a String* come in first place with forty-seven points, it had one of the widest margins of victory between first and second ever witnessed in the competition.

The funny thing with this song was that Shaw didn't really like the song. It was her least favourite of the five songs she performed for the Eurovision selection. In her own words she hated it for its sexist drivel and cuckoo-clock tune. Those views have mellowed in later years.

Also she was nearly dropped by the BBC as she was the "other woman" in a divorce case.

Shaw was the first artist to perform barefoot in the competition. She released *Puppet on a String* with the second placed selection song on the B side. The single reached number one in the singles charts and

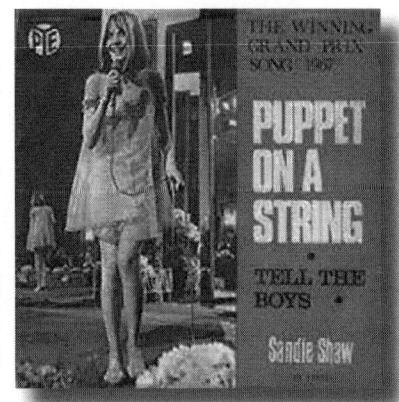

record sold in excess of 4,000 000 copies worldwide with over 1,000 000 in Germany alone and was the biggest selling single of the year. Also the biggest selling Eurovision single to date. It's estimated to be the biggest selling single by a British female artist of all time.

After the success of Eurovision Shaw went on to have her own fashion label. She also had her own TV show *The Sandie Shaw Supplement*. She had several hit records. In 1972 she retired from the life of being a pop singer and began working on other ventures, including writing musicals, songwriting and acting in stage productions.

But she will always be remembered as the girl in bare feet who achieved the UK's first win in Eurovision singing *Puppet on a String*, one of the most iconic Eurovision songs in UK Eurovision history, if not European Eurovision history.

Author's Comment:
Everybody loves Sandie Shaw and this is a Eurovision Classic!!!!

The Early Years

1968

Cliff Richard

Having won the previous year with Sandie Shaw's *Puppet on a String* the event was held at the Royal Albert Hall in London. A total of 17 countries participated and the contest was won by Spain with a song titled *La la la* by Massiel.

One note of interest with the winning song sung by Massiel is that he was not the original choice. It was due to be sung by Joan Manuel Serrat, but his demand to sing in his native Catalan was deemed to be an affront to the Francoist State dictatorship, so he was replaced by Massiel as a late replacement.

After the success of Shaw, the BBC wanted another big name to represent the UK and secure another win. Cilla Black was first choice but she decided against it as she believed there is no way the UK would secure back to back wins and she didn't want to damage her career with failure.

So, Cliff Richard (real name Harry Roger Webb) was chosen. He had dominated the UK charts in the 50s and early 60s with his backing group The Shadows and his rock and roll brand of music. He had also had success acting in several films. By 1968 his music had toned down from the earlier style and he was making a more middle of the road sound.

Once again the viewers chose their favourite out of five songs. The winning song with a landslide of votes was *Congratulations*.

Congratulations was the critics and bookmakers favourite to win the competition but unfortunately lost out to Spain by only one point with twenty-eight points.

The song was released as a single and topped the UK singles charts for two weeks. It is the first of only two Eurovision songs that has topped the charts without winning the competition.

The song was also one of fourteen songs chosen in 2005 by Eurovision fans to take part in an anniversary competition.

The UK in Eurovision - *The Highs and Lows*

Cliff Richard on stage during the Eurovision Song Contest rehearsals at the Royal Albert Hall, London, April 3rd, 1968.

Trinity Mirror / Mirrorpix / Alamy Stock Photo

The Early Years

The song was released in French, German, Italian and Spanish.

Surfacing in the media many years later in 2008, documentary filmmaker Montse Fernandex Vila allegedly claimed a Spanish journalist had said the 1968 Eurovision was rigged and that Franco had sent state officials across Europe offering cash bribes and promising to buy television series and contract unknown artists.

The allegation was based on a testimony by a TVE employee at the time, who claimed it was common knowledge, suggestions were made that Spanish record labels offered to release albums by Bulgarian and Czech artists, neither Czechoslovakia or Bulgaria were members of the EBU (European Broadcasting Union) at the time, although a Czech represented Austria. The documentary claimed the contest should have been won by the UK with *Congratulations*. Massiel (the winner) was outraged by the allegations and the scandal.

The journalist at the centre of the allegations has since said his words were misinterpreted by the documentary.

Losing the final didn't cause any harm to Cliff Richard's career, he has gone on to be one of the UK's most successful solo artists of all time. Having hit records in nearly every decade. Selling over 250 million records and sold-out tours worldwide.

Author's Comment:
Another Eurovision Classic, the song would have been a worthy winner, we shall never know if that documentary was accurate or not.

The UK in Eurovision - *The Highs and Lows*

1969

Lulu

This year's event took place at the Teatro Rea, in Madrid, Spain on 29th March. Sixteen countries took part, with Austria deciding not to take part, rumour had it was because they didn't want to take part in Francoist controlled Spain.

Spectacularly four countries were declared joint winners, the UK (we will get to that further down), The Netherlands with *De troubadour* sung by Lenny Kuhr, France with *Un jour, un enfant*, by Frida Boccara and Spain with *Vivo cantando* sung by Salomé. This was the first time in the history of the contest that a tie had occurred. As there was no tiebreaker rule in place in case of this happening, all four countries were declared winners. Spain becoming the first country in history to win back to back victories.

Now the UK entry was chosen once again by the BBC and they chose Scottish singer Lulu, real name Marie McDonald McLaughlin Lawrie. She had just secured a major hit in 1967 with the song *To Sir with Love* from the hit film with the same name.

She performed six songs and the winner *Boom Bang-a-Bang* written by Alan Moorhouse and Peter Warne was chosen as the winning song by the public.

As mentioned above she was a four-way winner with a joint score of eighteen points.

She released *Boom Bang-a-Bang* as single and it went to number two in the singles chart. This was her most successful ever hit in Britain. It was also a major hit throughout Europe and the song was also recorded in French, German, Italian and Spanish.

Lyrically the song is about her lover to "cuddle me tight", and her heart goes boom bang-a-bang when her lover is near.

Funnily, twenty years after the songs release, it was banned from BBC radio and TV playlists during the first Gulf war in 1991.

It was also chosen as the title of a one-hour show made to

The Early Years

Lulu, arriving at Barajas Airport, Madrid, accompanied by her husband, the Bee Gee Maurice Gibb.

celebrate 50 years of Eurovision and became the theme tune for the BBC sitcom *Him and Her* in 2010.

Lulu went onto have a successful career in music and TV and had her own TV series in 1968 through to 1975. She made several studio albums and in 2021 was awarded a CBE[1] in the honours list for her services to music.

Author's Comment:
Another Eurovision Classic performed by a music icon!

Lulu's song a Eurovision winner
by JOHN GALE

BRITAIN, France, the Netherlands, and Spain, all with 18 points, shared first prize in the fourteenth Eurovision Song Contest at Madrid last night.

Lulu, for Britain, managing to look both jolly and coy, wrinkling her nose and rolling her eyes, sang 'Boom-Bang-a-Bang,' a cheerful up-and-down song, with great professionalism.

Frida Boccara, of France, who had a splendid young-old face beneath black hair, sang with great feeling 'Un Jour, Un Enfant,' which was sad and romantic, in the French manner.

Lenny Kuhr, of the Netherlands, one of the composers of her song, 'De Troubadour,' accompanied herself on the guitar, and the style of her song was reminiscent of a French ballad. She had long brown hair and a pleasing simplicity.

Salome, of Spain, wearing a dress like white seaweed, sang 'Vivo Cantando' with energy and a certain amount of hip-waggling, putting everything she'd got into the last moments of her song.

The Observer, March 30th, 1969

---

1. Commander of the Order of the British Empire, the CBE is the highest ranking Order of the British Empire award.

The Early Years

LULU

Lulu's corny Eurovision song is a winner!

RAY CONNOLLY

If you follow the Top Ten every week, and if you watched that yawningly tedious Eurovision Song Contest last Saturday night, you will know that there is just no accounting for taste when it comes to pop music.

Before the show I wouldn't have given Lulu (much as I like her) a cat in hell's chance of being among the winners. But after having heard the other entries, I could have believed anything.

Still, she won, along with three other equally unmemorable songs.

But there's another way of looking at the four way win; could it be that all the songs were so poor that no single one emerged above the mediocrity of the others.

Biggest jump

Maybe all the songs were losers on Saturday night, but some lost a little more badly than others.

Anyway losers or not, Lulu and Boom Bang-A-Bang make inevitably the biggest charts jump of the week today and move upto number eight position in the Top Ten.

Like I say, there's no accounting for taste . . .

The full Top Ten according to the New Musical Express is (last week's positions in brackets):

1 (1), I Heard It Through The Grapevine: Marvin Gaye; 2 (3), Gentle On My Mind: Dean Martin; 3 (7), Sorry Suzanne: The Hollies; 4 (4), In The Bad, Bad Old Days: The Foundations; 5 (4), Surround Yourself With Sorrow: Cilla Black.

6 (2), Where Do You Go To: Peter Sarstedt; 7 (10), Games People Play: Joe South; 8 (18), Boom-Bang-A-Bang: Lulu; 9 (6), First Of May: The Bee Gees; and 10 (15), Get Ready: The Temptations.

Evening Standard, March 31st, 1969.

LULU—her husband can sing sweeter.

The farce of Eurovision's foursome

JUST who do they think they are? What are they trying to do? And if it goes "Boom Bang-a-Bang," who the heck cares?

So it just went "Boom Bang-a-Bang," and that was about all, and Lulu was just appalling, and it bores me to see praise heaped upon someone with such insincerity.

The Eurovision Song Contest has in its list of entries enough brainpower to knock the lid off pop music. Yet judges could not pick a winner.

Nobody worthy

Four songs were finally chosen as top. To me they could have chosen any of them. To me it was all outlandish bounding rubbish. If one winner cannot be picked, then nobody is worthy of winning, and nobody was. Like "Congratulations," Lulu's little effort was supposed to portray the bouncing, lively and carefree attitude of the British. Who's kidding who?

It meant nothing, and it was just a rollicking mass of brashness. Lulu is alive, but her husband can sing sweeter. It followed in the Cliff Richard pattern, and it was an insult to our music industry.

Methinks that when these songs are written for E.S.C., originality is forgotten. Writers and producers wrongly feel that to win you must enter a song acceptable in the latter half of a German beer festival.

We are the kings of the

by Roy Hollingworth

pop world, so why must we resort to the sound of a slightly merry brass band.

We must have a big punchy line, and smashing boppy chorus. Throw all we have produced in the last five years to the wind, and go back to the three-minute happy-go-lucky noise. I'm afraid that this is how it must happen.

To me, Lulu has only ever succeeded in presenting one number successfully, and that was "Shout." She had the voice for it.

Last year a superb female star arose. She was subtle and intelligent. But she was forgotten. Her name, Mary Hopkin, and she was ideal for the contest.

Derby Evening Telegraph, April 5th, 1969

*So at the end of the early years, 1956-1969, the UK has had a successful association with Eurovision.
With six second place finishes and two wins, that is some achievement.
A good decade!*

The 70s
1970-1979

1970

Mary Hopkin

New decade and the Eurovision circus moves onto the Netherlands at the RAI Congrescentrum, Amsterdam for the 15th Eurovision Song Contest, held on Saturday, 21st March.

Due to the fact that four countries tied for the winning song the previous year, it was taken in consideration that Spain had hosted in 1969 and the UK in 1968, so it left it between the Netherlands and France who would host and so lots were drawn and the Netherlands won.

Only 12 nations took part this year, the lowest number since 1959, Finland, Norway, Portugal, Sweden and Austria all boycotted this years competition — official reason given is they felt that the smaller nations were being marginalised and the competition favoured the larger nations and this no longer presented good television entertainment. It was also rumoured they were dissatisfied with the four-way tie result in 1969.

Ireland won the competition with the song *All Kinds of Everything* sung by Dana this was the first of Ireland's many victories and a fact worth mentioning, this was the only time Luxembourg received zero points.

Now the UK artist was internally chosen and Welsh singer-songwriter Mary Hopkin who had already had success with *Those Were the Days* and *Goodbye* was the preferred choice. She performed six shortlisted songs that were showcased one each week on the TV show *It's Cliff Richard*. The song the viewers finally picked to represent the UK was *Knock, Knock, Who's There?* Written by John Carter and Geoff Stevens. In the final she was backed by two backing singers John Evans and Brian Bennett.

In the run-up to the contest the UK was heavily backed to win. Being the favourites, and so sure of victory the UK delegation had organised a winner's party.

The UK in Eurovision - *The Highs and Lows*

During the voting there were only two countries in it — the UK and Ireland — the latter winning by six points.

One consolation for Hopkin was the song scored a number two hit in the UK charts and it became a hit across Europe and in 1972 also became a minor hit in the US.

She had a successful career and went on to have a few more hits but after getting married in 1971 she dropped out of the limelight and sometime later surprisingly she commented in an interview that her appearance in Eurovision was humiliating and that she hated the song she sung.

One very interesting fact from this year was the appearance of a little-known Spanish singer Julio Iglesias.

Author's Comment:
Not a classic by any means, Hopkin has a super voice, but I didn't agree with the favourite tag before the final but a worthy runner-up.

1971

Clodagh Rogers

Dublin, Ireland and the Gaiety Theatre on the 3rd April held this year's competition, with a total of 18 countries taking part.

Austria returned after a two-year absence and Finland, Norway, Portugal and Sweden also returned with Malta appearing for the first time.

The competition was won by Monaco with a song titled *Un banc, un arbre, une rue* performed by a French artist Séverine. This was the only time Monaco won. A quirky fact from this year, it was the only time the second and third placed entrants were awarded.

On another note for the first time groups of six people were allowed to perform, a break from the solo or duet format.

The UK entrant was chosen very carefully for this event. Due to the ongoing hostilities in Northern Ireland, the UK was worried about a backlash. So Northern Irish singer Clodagh Rogers was chosen. She was popular in both the UK and the Republic of Ireland.

She was best known as a singer and actress and for her hit singles *Come Back and Shake Me* and *Goodnight Midnight* from 1969.

The fact she was a Northern Irish girl didn't seem to appease the IRA[1] as she still received death threats for representing the UK.

Once again the winning song was chosen after six songs were performed by Rogers at the UK National Final which was shown on the *It's Cliff Richard* show and the winning song was *Jack In The Box* written by David Myers and composed by John Worsley.

Rogers performed at number nine in the final and had four backing singers, she came fourth in the competition with 98 points. This was the first time since 1966 that the UK had not been placed first or second.

The song was released as a single with the B-side one of the other performed songs, it reached number four in the UK charts and was actually Rogers last top ten hit in the UK. Despite the set back in Eurovision Rogers still had a successful career guesting on many TV

The UK in Eurovision - *The Highs and Lows*

shows and appearing in cabaret.

This year also marked the first year popular radio personality Terry Wogan began his long association with Eurovision.

Author's Comments:
Catchy song, and Clodagh put in a good performance. Finished in about the right position.

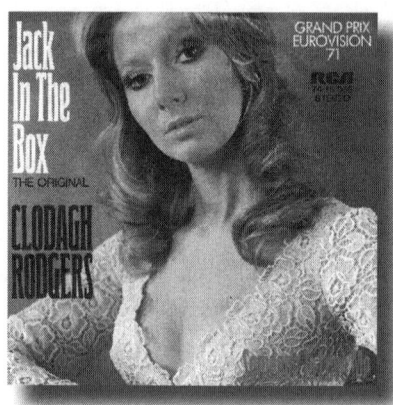

Will Clodagh leap to the top?

TONIGHT, the 1971 Eurovision Song Contest features songs and singers from 18 countries bidding to win the best-known song competition in the world, watched by the biggest single audience any of the artists is ever likely to have —about 50-million.

BBC-1 screens the whole contest live at 9.45 from the Gaiety Theatre, Dublin, as Clodagh Rodgers, singing ninth of the 18 singers, attempts to put Britain's 'Jack in the Box' top of the European pops.

What are her chances? As a girl the record favours her. No fewer than 11 of the 15 contests so far have been won by girl singers.

This year half the songs will be sung by girls, and five more by groups featuring girls.

As Britain's representative, Clodagh is a strong tip Britain has won the contest twice, and been second seven times.

Judging

There will be a big change in the method of voting the winner.

Instead of anonymous juries in capital cities, there will be only two jurymen from each coutry.

They will be in Dublin, and will be named and seen on screen. They will mark each song out of five points.

Evening Post,, April 3rd, 1971.

1.IRA stands for The Irish Republican Army ia name used by various paramilitary organisations in Ireland throughout the 20th and 21st centuries.

1972

The New Seekers

Monaco the winners the previous year found that they could not meet the demands of hosting the event after a suitable venue could not be found.

So once again the UK stepped in and Edinburgh was chosen, with the contest being held at the Usher Hall on 25th March. This is the one and only time when the UK has hosted the contest that it has been outside of England.

Eighteen countries took part, the same as the previous year. Luxembourg won with the song *Aprés Toi* performed by Vicky Leandros. A fact worth mentioning, the writer of the winning song Yves Dessca also wrote *Un Banc, Un Arbre* that had won in 1971 and thus became the second person to win the competition twice. The first person to win for two different countries and the first person to win two years in a row.

In the UK, media reports at the time suggested that the BBC had chosen Cliff Richard to represent the UK, but due to contractual commitments he was unavailable. The New Seekers were booked to appear on his TV series, so the BBC decided to offer them the opportunity. They were the first group to represent the UK.

They consisted of members Eve Graham, Lyn Paul, Marty Kristian, Peter Doyle and Paul Layton. They had just spent five weeks at Number two in the UK singles chart with *Never Ending Song of Love*. Just as it was announced they were chosen for Eurovision, their new song *I'd Like to Teach the World to Sing* hit number one in the UK singles charts and stayed there for four weeks. During this period the group began presenting the six short listed songs for the competition weekly on *The Cliff Richard Show*. Then a final show where they performed all six and after the public could vote for their favourite, albeit by post.

The winning song was *Beg, Steal or Borrow*, written by Tony

Cole, Steve Wolfe and Graeme Hall.

The song was heavily favoured by the critics to win, and after a good performance by the group in the Eurovision final it was a disappointment that they came home in second place with 114 points, only fourteen points behind winners Luxembourg.

The song was released as a single with the runner up song as the B-side and it reached number two in the charts. It was also included on their LP *We'd Like To Teach the World to Sing* and this also reached number two in the UK album chart.

Author's Comment:
Great song, great performance. In my opinion it should have won.

The 70s

1973

Cliff Richard

This year's competition took place at the Grand Théatre on 7th April in Luxembourg City, Luxembourg.

Seventeen countries took part with Austria and Malta deciding not to participate with Israel stepping in for the first time.

The host nation took the honours with back to back victories with the song *Tu te reconnaitras* performed by Anne-Marie David with a winning total of 129 points. The voting was very close with Spain finishing only four points behind.

This was the highest score achieved in Eurovision under any voting format until 1975. The winning song took a maximum of eighty-one percent, but the scoring system this year guaranteed at least two points to every country from every country voting.

Also this year the rule of countries singing in their national language was abolished, so some countries decided to sing in English.

Due to action of terrorists at the 1972 Munich Olympics, security was duly tightened due to the participation of Israel.

A quote that was often spoken of by Terry Wogan when talking about this Eurovision final was the floor manager of the event requested that the audience remained seated when applauding the contestants due to the fear of being shot by security.

Another fact is that this year's competition also holds the record for the most watched Eurovision song contest in the UK with over 23.54 million viewers, a million more than the previous year, this was the most watched programme in the UK in 1973.

Now the UK entry was again chosen internally and for the second time Cliff Richard was chosen to represent the UK.

Six songs were performed on the BBC Cilla Black television series *Cilla*. The winning song was chosen by viewers sending in their vote by post card and overwhelmingly the winning song was *Power to All Our Friends* written by Doug Flett and Guy Fletcher.

The UK in Eurovision - *The Highs and Lows*

Once again Cliff was denied the success of winning, by only coming third, this was a big disappointment to Cliff and the UK selection board.

The song itself was released as a single and reached number four in the UK charts, his first top five hit since *Congratulations* in 1968 and his last hit until 1979. The song was also released in French, German and Spanish versions.

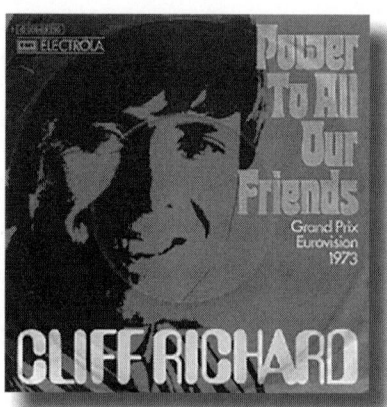

Worth mentioning for the die-hard UK Eurovision fans, this was the first contest that Terry Wogan commentated on for BBC TV, having previously broadcasted only on the radio.

Author's Comment:
Quality song by a top artist, disappointing result, another year where the UK was definitely good enough to have won.

Sunday Mirror, April 8th, 1973.

The 70s

1974

Olivia Newton-John

Before we begin, at the age of twelve this was my first real taste of Eurovision, I remember watching with my parents and loving every minute of it, from the performances, the outfits, and the most exciting of all, the scoring.

Right let's get started. After Luxembourg won the contest in 1972 and 1973 they declined to host it again due to financial reasons. So the UK stepped in once again, the Brighton Dome was chosen to host the 19th contest on 6th April.

Seventeen countries took part with France being absent this year and Greece competing for the first time.

In my opinion, this year's result saw the biggest winners the competition has ever had — although at the time they were unknowns — of course I am referring to ABBA with *Waterloo*. Every time that song is played I still see that performance in Brighton in my head. I was mesmerised from the moment they took the stage.

We all know that after this competition Abba went onto be one of the biggest selling artists of all time.

The UK entry this year was again picked by the BBC. Olivia Newton-John, although an Australian, she had been living in the UK for a few years. The same format for the winning song was chosen whereby she performed six different songs and the most popular song was chosen by the viewers, this time all six songs were performed on Jimmy Savile's *Clunk Click* show.

The winning chosen song was *Long Live Love*. The artist and song were considered to be strong contenders and favourite with many of the bookmakers for this year's competition but as usual that doesn't mean much. She took to the stage with five backing singers and finished in joint fourth place with Luxembourg and Monaco with fourteen points.

The UK in Eurovision - *The Highs and Lows*

After the show Olivia commented that she wasn't happy with the song that had been chosen for her to sing.

A few newspapers reported this the morning after the final.

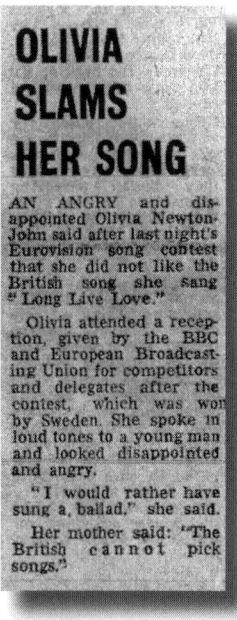

Sunday Sun,
April 7th, 1974.

Cambridge Evening News,
April 8th, 1974.

As in the past the winning song was released as a single and peaked at number eleven in the UK charts. It charted at eleven in her native Australia. It was also released throughout mainland Europe but only really had any decent chart success in Norway.

One little note of interest is that Olivia was the last solo artist to represent the UK until 1985.

August 22nd, 2022 Eurovision's official YouTube channel uploaded the Brighton performance in tribute to Olivia after her death.

Author's Comment:
Agree with Olivia, awful and definitely the wrong song for her. If it wasn't for the fact that she was a terrific artist and did actually put in a good performance, I would have scored the song one point.

The 70s

UK Evening Argus, March 30th, 1974

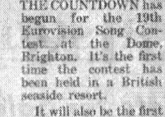

1975

The Shadows

Held at Stockholmsmässan, Stockholm, Sweden on 22nd March, nineteen countries took part, with France and Malta returning after one and two year absences. Turkey made its debut and Greece declined after its debut year last year.

The winner was the Netherlands with a song titled *Ding-a-dong* performed by Teach-In.

Security was tightened at this year's event after reports of a possible terrorist attack by the Red Army Faction, but it was the West German embassy that was hit a month later.

The lead up to the contest was also plagued by protests from the Swedish left movement against the contest and the commercial aspect of it. This would have repercussions in 76.

The UK choice this year was also controversial. The Shadows were the chosen act by the BBC. This led to widespread condemnation from the music writers, media and general public. Calls were made for the Music writers, composers to chose the artist and the songs.

The group was made up of members Bruce Welch, John Farrar, Hank Marvin and Brian Bennett.

A low postal vote did indeed persuade the BBC that a new format was needed.

Members of the group were responsible for two of the six shortlisted songs being performed, this again led to condemnation from the music publishers associations. The six songs were performed on the BBC series *Lulu*. The winning song had the lowest number of votes ever recorded for a UK selection final. That song being *Let Me Be the One*.

Surprisingly, the song finished a credible second place in the Eurovision final with a points tally of 138.

Again the winning song was released as a single and reached a credible number twelve in the charts, their first hit since 1967.

The writer of the winning song Paul Curtis went onto be the most successful writer in the history of the UK selection process, he wrote a further twenty-one songs that reached the UK finals.

Author's Comment:
Can't see what all the fuss was about with the critics, it was pleasing that they were proved wrong, I liked it.

The UK in Eurovision - *The Highs and Lows*

Brotherhood are tops

BRITAIN'S chart-topping pop group, Brotherhood of Man, were on top of the world last night after winning the Eurovision Song Contest.

The group — two men and two girls, pictured above — beat challengers from 17 other countries to scoop first place.

The international panel of judges had no hesitation in voting for Brotherhood's catchy number Save Your Kisses For Me.

The British group finished with 164 points. France was second with 147.

Millions of British television viewers joined those from 25 other countries to watch the contest, which was broadcast live from The Hague.

The group's success last night is an extra boost for their song — which has topped the British charts for the past two weeks.

Their recording of it has already sold 350,000 copies — and looks like earning Brotherhood their first gold disc.

Strangely enough, the song was originally written for last year's Eurovision contest.

Explained the group's lead singer, Martin Lee, who also helped write the song: "We didn't think it was good enough last year.

"So we revamped it and submitted it for this year's contest."

For the first time in the contest's 21 years Sweden was not represented.

Swedish TV officials said last October that the contest, sponsored by the European Broadcasting Union, had degenerated in quality

Sunday Mirror, April 4th, 1976

1976

The 70s

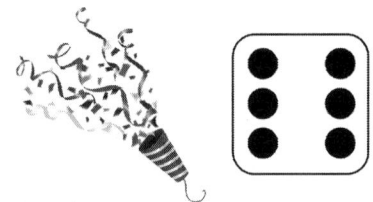

Brotherhood of Man

The Congrescentrum, The Hague, Netherlands hosted the 21st edition of the contest on April 3rd. Eighteen countries participated with Sweden, Malta and Turkey opting out this year with Malta not participating again until 1991. Greece and Austria both returned.

This was a triumphant year for the UK, they won the competition with the song *Save Your Kisses For Me*, written by Tony Hiller, Lee Sheriden and Martin Lee and by the group Brotherhood of Man, which consisted of members Martin Lee, Nicky Stevens, Sandra Stevens and Lee Sheriden.

After the debacle and criticism the previous year with the lowest published figure for the public voting in the UK finals after the BBC's choice of The Shadows. It led to an all-comers final being reinstated, the format used for the UK finals from 1961-1963. Twelve songs were chosen by the Music Publisher's Association, with the songwriters choosing their own artist. The Final took place at the Royal Albert Hall and fourteen regional juries voted on the songs. They were ranked 1-12 with twelve points awarded to the favourite, *Save Your Kisses for Me* won and went on to win the Eurovision final.

A few records were broken with this song. Firstly it was released as a single and went to Number 1. It was the biggest selling single of 1976 in the UK and the sixth biggest selling single of the 1970s in the UK with sales in excess of one million. Globally it sold over six million copies making it the biggest selling winning single in the history of the Eurovision Song Contest.

Another record was the 164 points scored out of a possible maximum of 204, the highest relative score ever reached under the Douze Points voting system inaugurated in 1975 and used ever since, with over 80% of the possible score attained. No song has achieved this since.

The song was selected as one of the entries for the 2005 Congratulations 50th anniversary special.

The UK in Eurovision - *The Highs and Lows*

Several other artists have released cover versions of the song including a country version by Margo Smith who had a major hit with it in the same year. The group have also re-recorded the single a couple of times. They went on to have other hit records in the years following their triumph in Europe.

They were still performing right up until December 2022 when they announced their retirement.

Author's Comment:
Eurovision Legends and an absolute classic Eurovision song!

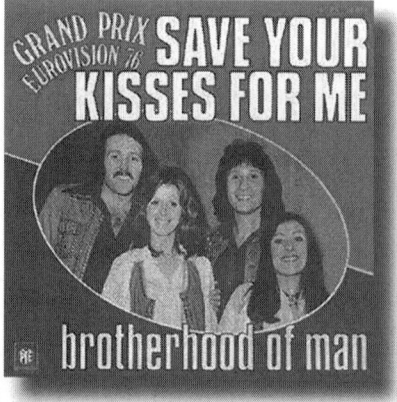

1977

Lynsey DePaul & Mike Moran

After Brotherhood of Man's win the previous year, London and the Wembley Conference Centre was the venue for the 22nd Eurovision Contest which took place on May 7th, the first time it was held in May since the very first contest in 1956.

The contest had been planned to take place on April 2nd, but due to the technicians being out on strike it was held back until the dispute was over.

Eighteen countries took part with Sweden returning and Yugoslavia opting out.

France was the winner on the day with a song called *L'Oiseau et l'Enfant*, sung by Marie Myriam.

The UK entry was chosen using the same selection format as the previous year, a winning song was chosen from a selection of twelve songs performed by different acts.

Just before the UK selection final was to be broadcast the TV technicians went on strike preventing the filming. The contest went ahead a few hours later but could only be broadcast on BBC Radio 2.

The winning entry chosen by regional panels was a song called *Rock Bottom* performed by Lynsey de Paul and Mike Moran.

Lynsey de Paul was a successful artist and song writer and the song *Rock Bottom* she co wrote with Mike Moran and she became the first female artist to perform her own song at Eurovision.

The song was favourite to win the contest. The BBC hadn't given its full support to the song as the corporation didn't want to win, as that would have required it to host the competition two years running. To the BBC's relief the song finished in second place.

A documentary that was aired many years later in 2022 confirmed the above that the BBC did not want to win the competition.

Rock Bottom was released as a single and reached number nineteen in the charts, the last chart hit Lynsey de Paul would achieve in the UK.

The song also top the charts in Switzerland, was number two in Austria, number four in Germany, number six in Sweden, number seven in Ireland and Norway and number eight in Belgium, and finally number ten in Israel and France.

Author's Comment:
Class number, great performance, and the entry of the conductor Ronnie Hazlehurst in a suit and bowler hat carrying a newspaper to complement the duo performing was genius. Shame it didn't win, would have been interesting to see the meltdown at the BBC.

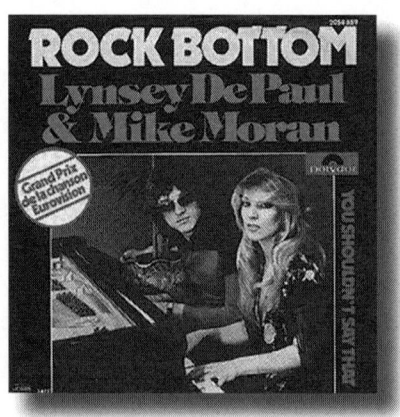

1978

Co-Co

Once again we are back in France, in Paris at the Palais des Congrès on 22nd April for the 23rd edition of Eurovision.

Twenty countries participated for the first time, the highest number up to this date. Denmark were making their long awaited return after twelve years and Turkey joined in again.

Winning entry was Israel with a song titled *A-Ba-Ni-Bi* performed by Izhar Cohen & the Alphabeta. This was the first time the winning song was performed in one of the Semitic languages. Also another first, it was the first Eurovision song to be conducted by a woman.

Norway finished last for the fifth time. But this time, and as we see later, by no means the last time, but the first country to receive "nul" points after the new voting system which was implemented in 1975.

Just to clarify, they were not in fact the first country to receive nul points, that was Portugal in 1964, but that was with the older voting system.

The selection of the UK entry went through the usual channels, twelve songs by different artists judged by regional juries. The winning song was *Bad Old Days* written by Stephanie de Sykes and Stuart Slater performed by the group Co-Co, who were Terry Bradford, Josie Andrews, Cheryl Baker, Keith Hasler and Paul Rogers.

It was the worst showing at the Eurovision up to this date, finishing a disappointing eleventh place with sixty-one points, and the first time a UK entry had not received a maximum or a ten points score from any of the juries.

The song was released as a single and peaked at number thirteen in the singles chart. It was the group's only ever hit.

Interesting and worth mentioning was that one of the performing group members of Co-Co this year was a certain Cheryl Baker who would be very prominent and go on to feature in Eurovision a few years later.

The 70s

Author's Comment:
One to forget!

The Rogers family groups round the television at the women's hospital in Sparkhill, Birmingham, where they will watch Paul Rogers, with Co-Co, in tonight's Eurovision Song Contest. Mr. Fred Rogers and his wife, Margaret, are pictured with daughters Mandy (left) and Lynda.

Family cross fingers for Co-Co star Paul

FINGERS crossed for Co-Co!

Tonight's Eurovision song contest has a special meaning for a Birmingham family.

For one of the singers with Co-Co, the group who shot to the top to represent Britain with the catchy song "The Bad Old Days" is their son, 21-year-old Paul.

"I am probably more nervous than he is," said mum, 42-year-old secretary, Mrs. Margaret Rogers, of Sylvia Avenue, West Heath.

At the moment she is a patient in the women's hospital in Showell Green Lane, Sparkhill, where she plans to watch the contest with her decorator husband, Derek, and daughters Lynda,

aged 20, and 14-year-old Mandy.

And from Paris where he is enjoying his stay in the £80-a-night Hotel Concorde Lafayette, ex-Bournville College schoolboy Paul confirmed that the six-man group is in good spirits.

"We are here to win and are looking forward to the finals," said the 5ft. 8in. blue-eyed pop star.

Birmingham Evening Mail, 22nd April, 1978

1979

Black Lace

The 24th Song Contest took place at the International Convention Centre, Jerusalem in Israel on 31st March.

Nineteen countries taking part, with only Turkey withdrawing after political pressure from Arab countries because of political pressure due to the Palestine/Israeli conflict.

For the second year in a row Israel won the competition with a song titled *Hallelujah* performed by Israeli group Milk and Honey featuring Gali Atari. This went on to be a huge international hit.

Before we go to the UK entry, one note of interest is that due to Israel not having broadcast in colour before they had to borrow cameras from the BBC.

Once again the UK selected winning song came through a national song contest where twelve artists performed. The final was due to be broadcast from the Royal Albert Hall on 8th March, but again a technicians strike stopped the show, so audio recordings of the songs were voted for by the regional juries.

The chosen song was *Mary Ann* written by Peter Morris and performed by Black Lace who were Alan Barton, Colin Routh, Terry Dobson and Steve Scholey.

The choice of winning song was controversial as the then successful band Smokie felt that the song was a rip-off of their song titled *Oh Carol* and their publishers threatened to take legal action, but the case was dropped.

According to the Black Lace camp there was no hiding the secret that they wanted to sound as near as possible to Smokie from vocal harmonies to guitars to drums. One of the Black Lace band members was quoted as allegedly saying it was an intentional rip-off.

The band performed seventeenth place in the final and was leading the competition at one stage but finally ended up seventh place in the field of nineteen with a score of seventy-three points.

The usual single was released and reached a high of forty-two in the charts, this being the lowest placing of an Eurovision entry for several years.

Black Lace needed not to have worried though as they would go on to have one of their biggest ever hits in the 80s with the pub and club classic *Agadoo*.

Author's Comment:
Definitely a rip-off! Nevertheless a catchy song.

Western Daily Press, 9th March, 1979

*So we come to the end of another decade,
1970-1979,
not quite the same success as the early
years, but still a few really good songs and
performances to remember with four second
place finishes and one winner!*

The 80s
1980-1989

1980

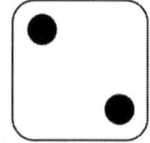

Prima Donna

Due to Israel declining to host the competition two years in a row, the Netherlands agreed to step-in and stage the event in The Hague at the Nederlands Congresgebouw on 19th April.

Nineteen countries participated with Monaco and the winning country from last year Israel deciding not to take part, Turkey made its return and Morocco made its only ever appearance in the competition.

The winner of the contest was Ireland with *What's Another Year*, performed by "Mr Eurovision" Johnny Logan. Coincidentally this was the second time Ireland had won the competion and as with the first time, it was in the Netherlands. This was also the first time a solo vocalist had won the competition since 1966.

The UK "A song for Europe" contest was held on 26th March, the usual twelve songs were chosen by the Music Publishers Association and twelve regional juries voted on a winner. One of the selected songs was disqualified two weeks before the final as the artists The New Seekers began promoting the single before the contest.

There was a tiebreak for the winning song and due to a shortage of time the twelve juries were hastily asked to pick their favourite between the two tiebreakers, Prima Donna and Maggie Moone. Funnily enough a few of the juries changed their original voting and switched to *Love Enough for Two* performed by Prima Donna. The whole scoring process descended into chaos and in the end Prima Donna won by eight votes to six.

The group was made up of sisters Kate Robbins and Jane Robbins, Sally Ann Triplett, Danny Finn, Alan Coates and Lance Aston (brother of Jay Aston who we will come to shortly), and the song *Love Enough for Two* was about love between two people and was written by Stuart Slater and Stephanie de Sykes.

At the Eurovision final the song finished a very creditable third place with 106 points.

The song was released as a single and was the first release since 1964 not to chart prior to a Eurovision final. It did eventually peak at number forty-eight in the UK singles chart.

Author's Comment:
Catchy tune, but not the most scintillating start to the new decade.

The UK in Eurovision - *The Highs and Lows*

BUCKS FIZZ IS THE TOP POP!

British victory in song contest

By TONY BUSHBY

BUBBLING Bucks Fizz made it a champagne party for Britain in the Eurovision Song Contest last night.

In sparkling style they beat 19 other nations in Dublin with their song Making Your Mind Up.

Germany's Johnny Blue and Lena Valaitis were second, and French entry Jean Gabilou was third.

Bucks Fizz—Bobby Gee, Mike Nolan, Jay Aston and Cheryl Baker—were teamed up specially for the contest. Their song is already riding high in the British charts.

And it clearly just had the edge — giving Britain their first Eurovision win for five years.

But the juries took their time making their minds up in a nail-biting finish.

Britain, France, Switzerland and Germany were all in the running until near the end.

Bucks Fizz finally clinched it with 136 points—4 points clear.

But if Britain was bubbling last night the Norwegians were feeling out in the cold.

Their entry, sung by Finn Kalik, didn't score a single point.

The contest was seen live by around 500 million TV viewers throughout Europe.

What the viewers did not see was the massive security cordon thrown around Dublin's Royal Society showgrounds where the contest was held.

Armed Special Branch detectives mingled with invited guests. And hundreds of Euro delegates had to pass through strict security checks before taking their seats.

Outside, pickets demonstrating over conditions in the H-Blocks of Ulster's Maze Prison, handed out leaflets.

Fizzing . . . Mike, Jay, Bobby and Cheryl

Sunday Mirror, 5th April, 1981

1981

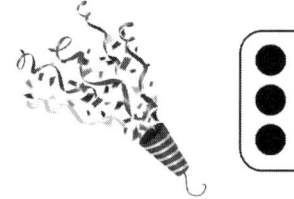

Bucks Fizz

The 26th Eurovision took place in Dublin, Ireland at RDS Simmonscourt on the 4th April.

Twenty countries took part equalling the record set in 1975. Cyprus made its first appearance this year whilst Yugoslavia and Israel both returned. Morocco and Italy decided against participation this year, as referenced earlier Morocco never returned and its only ever appearance was in 1980.

The winner was United Kingdom with the song *Making Your Mind Up* performed by Bucks Fizz, with a points tally of 136, four points clear of Germany second and France third. Norway once again received nul points, the third time in Eurovision.

The UK entry was once again chosen after the usual *A Song for Europe* final which was held on 11th March, Bucks Fizz were the winners from a field of eight other artists.

Bucks Fizz were only formed a couple of months before the UK *Song for Europe* final. The song was written by Andy Hill and Bucks Fizz consisted of members Bobby G, Mike Nolan, Jay Aston, Cheryl Baker. As we mentioned previously the brother of Jay Aston represented the UK in last years final, also Cheryl Baker had also represented the UK in 1978 in the group Co-Co.

The performance during the final was criticised as being off-key and led to reports that they were chosen more for their looks than genuine vocal ability. The performance is best remembered for the moment when the two male singers rip the skirts off the girls to reveal shorter skirts, some believe this gimmick swung the voting in their favour. Years later Cheryl Baker commented that their poor performance was due to nerves and Mike Nolan also quoted that the microphones had got mixed up when setting up the gear.

The famous skirt routine has been copied in later Eurovision finals most notably for Latvia when they won in 2002.

The UK in Eurovision - *The Highs and Lows*

The song was released as a single and reached number one in the UK where it stayed for three weeks, it also made the charts and reached number one in several other European countries, it sold in excess of four million copies.

The success at Eurovision was the launch pad that turned the group into one of the biggest selling artists of the 1980s.

To this day *Making Your Mind Up* is regarded as one of the classic Eurovision pop songs.

Author's Comment:
When anybody mentions Eurovision, Bucks Fizz and Making Your Mind Up is one of the songs that always comes to mind, what a legacy!

The 80s

1982

Bardo

Harrogate International Centre, Harrogate, UK was the venue for the 27th edition of Eurovision on the 24th April. A total of eighteen countries took part, noted absentees this year were Greece and France, who lost the rights to participate this year due to the downsizing of their national broadcasters.

The winning song was Germany's *Ein bißchen Frieden* sung by Nicole. This was the first time Germany had won, they had competed at every final since the start in 1956.

The song received 1.61 times as many votes as the second placed Israel, a record under the current scoring system, which stood until 2009.

At the end of competition Nicole sung an English version of the song which translated means *A Little Bit of Peace* to the delight of the audience. This subsequently went straight to Number one in the UK singles charts.

This year's UK entry went through the usual *Song for Europe* selection final that was held on 24th March.

The winning entry was *One Step Further* written by Simon Jeffries and performed by Bardo, who were a duo of Sally Ann-Triplett and Stephen Fischer. They were formed specifically to enter the Eurovision Song Contest.

Sally Ann-Triplett became only the third singer to win the UK *Song for Europe* twice, having won in 1980 as part of the group Prima Donna. Cliff Richard has represented the UK twice but on those occasions he hadn't had to go through a selection process.

Bardo were the bookmakers favourites to win the competition. They performed fourth on the night. Critics complained that their performance was littered with nerves and more attention was paid to the dance routine than to their singing. That could account for why they came a disappointing seventh place with seventy-six points.

The UK in Eurovision - *The Highs and Lows*

The song did fair much better in the UK singles charts and peaked at number two, it received a silver disc with sales of over 250,000. It was the seventy-fifth best-selling single in the UK in 1982.

Author's Comment:
I like One Step Further, *a cheesy dance routine from the duo, but a catchy song.*

Bardot take it one step further

by ROY GILLARD

If the British duo, Bardot win next week's Eurovision Song Contest, among those they will have to thank are last year's winners, Bucks Fizz.

For the song that Bardot will sing One Step Further was written for Bucks Fizz to sing.

It was offered to their producer, Andy Hill, who decided it had considerable Eurovision potential.

So as Bucks Fizz were not in this year's contest, Bardot were given the chance to sing it. They won the British finals.

Bucks Fizz think that Bardot have "a very good chance" of winning the contest for Britain for the second year.

"It's a great song and we thought Bardot did very well with it in the British finals," said Michael Nolan.

the unmarried male member of the group.

"We would almost certainly have included the song in our new LP, Are You Ready? if it had not been chosen for Eurovision", Michael said.

Incidentally, despite the same surname, Michael, is not a brother of the Nolan sisters.

Bucks Fizz were at the Night Out, Birmingham, at the weekend — just

one year after winning the 1981 contest.

Their Eurovision winner, "Making Your Mind Up" topped the charts for them. But since then they have had four more big chart successes.

Apart from Abba, they have almost certainly already become more successful than any other previous Eurovision winner.

Spot the spelling mistake from the Birmingham Evening Post, 13th April 1982.

1983

Sweet Dreams

Rudi-Sedlmayer-Halle, Munich, West Germany held the 28th Eurovision Song Contest on 23rd April. There were twenty countries participating with France, Greece and Italy all returning and Ireland opting out due to workers industrial action.

The winning country was Luxembourg with a song titled *Si la vie est cadeau* performed by Corinne Hermes, this was Luxembourg's fifth win, matched only by that of France.

There were also a couple of nul points this year that being Spain and Turkey.

A special point worth mentioning, this was the first year the event was televised in Australia.

A Song for Europe show was the usual selection for the UK entry, and this year a song titled *I'm Never Giving Up* was the winning entry written and composed by Ron Roker, Jan Pulsford, and Phil Wigger and performed by Sweet Dreams.

The group was a trio made-up of Bobby McVay, Carrie Gray and Helen Kray, the song was about never giving up in their quest for winning back their lover.

They performed first during the final and the group used stools as props and the up-tempo song finished a credible sixth place in the final with seventy-nine points.

The released single peaked at number twenty-one after spending eight weeks in the UK charts.

That was the trio's only hit and they disbanded later that year.

Author's Comment:
Nice up-tempo song is about all you can say about it.

1984

Belle and the Devotions

Luxembourg City and the Théatre Municipal, Luxembourg staged this years 29th contest on the 5th May.

A total of Nineteen countries took part, Israel opted out due to the date conflicting with the country's Yom HaZikaron[1] holiday.

The winner this year was Sweden with a song titled *Diggi-Loo Diggi-Ley* performed by Herreys. (This was the first winning song in Swedish, Abba had performed Waterloo in English).

Worth mentioning before we tackle the UK entry is that Herreys was made up of three brothers and two members of the group remain the youngest male winners of the competition.

The UK entry was chosen through the usual *A Song for Europe* selection process. The winning entry was *Love Games* performed by Belle and the Devotions. Two of the acts they were up against were Hazel Dean and Sinitta who we know went on to be successful chart acts under the guidance of Stock Aitken & Waterman.

Belle and the Devotions was made up of Kit Rolfe, Laura James and Linda Sofield. The song *Love Games* was composed and written by Paul Curtis. The 1960s Motown sounding melody finished in seventh place with sixty-three points. This was the third worst performing UK entry since 1957.

There was a bit of controversy during and after Belle and the Devotions had finished their performance in the final. They were met with boos from the audience. Apparently this was a reaction to the riot by English football fans the previous November when England were knocked out of the European Championship.

The Dutch delegation also lodged a complaint as the backing singers who were performing the song were hidden and not seen by the TV viewers, whereas Laura James and Linda Sofield were miming their vocals. The BBC insisted that this was because one of the backing singers was pregnant.

The 80s

Kit Rolfe had in fact been involved in Eurovision the year before. He had been hidden off camera when providing backing vocals for Sweet Dreams.

The song was released as a single and didn't do too badly it reached number eleven in the UK singles charts.

Author's Comment:
A Supremes *rip-off! I liked it, not out of place at Wigan Casino.*

Sunday Mirror, 6th May, 1984

---

1. Memorial Day for the Fallen Soldiers of the Wars of Israel and Victims of Actions of Terrorism enacted into law in 1963

1985

Vikki

Sweden, Gothenburg and the Scandinavium was the venue on the 4th May with nineteen countries taking part with the Netherlands and Yugoslavia deciding not to participate.

Netherlands opting out because of their remembrance day and Yugoslavia because of the anniversary of the death of former president Tito[2].

The winning entry was Norway this year with a song titled *La det swinge* performed by the duo Bobbysocks. This was Norway's first victory, and preceded a long period of low scores which included nul points on three occasions.

The 1985 UK *Song for Europe* was held at the BBC TV studios on 9th April, the winning was *Love Is...*, written and composed by James Kaleth and Vikki Watson and performed by Vikki Watson, just using her first name as her artist name.

She was the first solo female vocalist to represent the UK since Olivia Newton-John in 1974 and only the second female composer to sing her composition at a final since Lynsey de Paul.

The song is a contemporary ballad is about a couple who are too afraid to fall head-first in love.

She performed in 14th place in the final and finished in fourth place with a credible 100 points, which is reasonable considering she didn't receive any twelve point hauls from any of the juries.

Despite the relative success in Gothenbourg the song only reached a disappointing number forty-nine in the UK singles charts.

Author's Comment:
Nice song, confident and well performed by Vikki. Worthy fourth place.

---

2. Yugoslav communist revolutionary, statesman, and later a dictator serving in various positions of national leadership from 1943 until his death in 1980.

1986

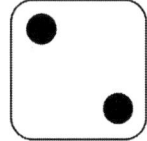

Ryder

The 31st edition of Eurovision was held in Bergen, Norway at the Grieghallen on 3rd May, with twenty countries taking part. Greece and Italy opting out and Yugoslavia and the Netherlands returning, with Iceland competing for the very first time.

Belgium ran out winners with a song titled *J'aime la vie* by Sandra Kim. Belgium was the last of the original seven countries that took part from 1956 to win Eurovision.

Aged 13 Kim was the youngest ever Eurovision winner, current rules now state participants to be at least sixteen years-old, so unless this rule is relaxed Kim's record will always stand. Before the contest Kim had stated that she was fifteen but after it was revealed that she was in fact only thirteen. Switzerland who finished second appealed for her to be disqualified, but the result stood.

This year marked the first time that royalty were present at a Eurovision final and those being the Norwegian Royal Family.

The UK entry chosen through *A Song for Europe* was the group Ryder with a song titled *Runner in the Night*.

Ryder was purposely created especially for the Eurovision entry this year. They were made up of six members, Maynard Williams, Dudley Phillips, Paul Robertson, Andy Ebsworth, Geoff Leach and Rob Terry. The song was composed by Brian Wade and lyrics by Maureen Darbyshire.

The song was a contemporary rock song with the group playing their own instruments without the need of an orchestra, the song itself is about a man running in the night to a woman he had previously left, hoping he isn't too late. Critics slammed the song as weak and totally inappropriate for Eurovision, they were not proved wrong.

Ryder finished in seventh place with 72 points, it only reached 98 in the UK singles charts, this was the worst for a Eurovision entry since 1964.

The UK in Eurovision - *The Highs and Lows*

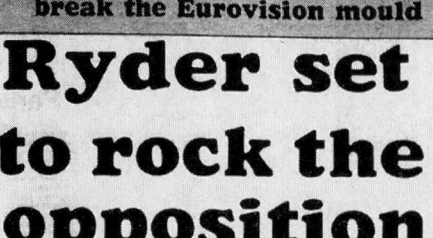

Ryder set to rock the opposition

The band who carry our hopes break the Eurovision mould

By MICHAEL BURKE

The typical "Boom-Bang-a-Bang" British Eurovision entries of the past have been shot to pieces by this year's surprising selection — a raunchy rock song.

As the countdown begins to Saturday's Eurovision battle, for the first time in years it seems Britain's bid by new group Ryder could be right on target to restore the nation's Eurovision song pride.

The recent singalong formula, two pretty boys in satin trousers and two pretty girls in tight skirts, has taken a back seat to Britain's rock entry, *Runner in the Night*.

Ryder's lead singer, Maynard Williams, son of comedian Bill Maynard, was optimistic today about the group's chances:

"We've got faith in the song. It's not the usual singalong stuff, but it has a strong melody put to a heavy rock backing. It's different enough and, in my opinion, it's good enough to win."

Ryder's keyboard player and backing vocalist Rob Terry, from Birmingham, was optimistic, too.

Speaking from his London flat, where nerves were starting to creep in, Rob said: "To be honest I thought we didn't have a chance of winning.

"I though some of the other entries were better, but now I'm more confident and I think we can do it," said Rob.

Tuning in

If Ryder make it in this 31st Eurovision Song Contest they will be the first British winners since Bucks Fizz in 1981.

More than 500 million viewers throughout Europe will be tuning in to the competition on Saturday night.

Terry Wogan has been looking forward to hosting the event once again, but he believes the appeal of the programme has little, if anything to do with the music.

"It's all down to Hillbilly rivalry. The attraction for families as far apart as the Algarve and Istanbul is based on patriotic support for their national team.

"In that sense it's the musical equivalent of the World Cup — never mind the football, are we winning?"

Terry also said that all eyes will again be on host country Norway, who finally scored some points last year — and won.

The writer of our entry this year, Maureen Derbyshire, is well aware of the fact that we haven't opted for the usual formula:

"In the past the winners have fitted into a specific category, but there's no formula about Ryder.

"The song will either sink, because it doesn't sound Eurovision enough, or will succeed because it has a fresh rock feel, which, ironically, is most popular with the European record-buying public."

With Ryder, there is certainly a big swing from the cutey-pie dance routines, the sequins and the toothy smiles. Ryder don't have it, but how much does that image count for?

T-shirts

"Ryder would normally get on stage in jeans, T-shirts and leather jackets. That wouldn't be right for Eurovision, but dressing everybody up in gimmicky gear isn't the answer either.

"Ryder will present a fashionable appearance, but we hope the song, not the look, will be the deciding factor," said Maureen.

In all, Britain has won four Eurovisions — Sandie Shaw in 1967, Lulu in 1969, Brotherhood of Man in 1976.

Birmingham Evening Mail, April 29th, 1986

Ryder: Britain's hopes in this year's Eurovision Song Contest.

Author's Comment:
Not convinced a contemporary rock song was a good idea in 1986.

1987

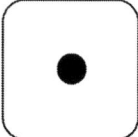

Rikki

After Belgium's first ever win, Brussels and the Centenary Palace was the chosen venue, twenty-two countries taking part, the highest number of countries up to this date, with Greece and Italy returning.

There was a bit a row between the BBC and the Belgium broadcasters, who were going to broadcast with the names of the sponsors on screen, something the BBC isn't permitted to do, so there were two official versions of the event made available, one with advertisers and one without.

The winning country was Ireland with a song titled *Hold Me Now* and sung by "Mr Eurovision himself" Johnny Logan. He won in competition in 1980, and to this date he still remains the only artist to have won the competition twice. I have a feeling that this could be matched this year in Liverpool with the Swedish entry, we will see.

The UK entry was chosen through the usual channel of *A Song for Europe* on 10th April by regional juries. *Only the Light* was the winning song written and performed by Rikki real name Richard Peebles.

Unfortunately *Only the Light* finished a lowly 13th place in the final with forty-seven points, it was the worst placed entry up to this date and remained the worst up until the year 2000.

To make matters worse for Rikki it only made ninety-six in the UK singles chart.

Author's Comment:
A song and a year to forget!

The UK in Eurovision - *The Highs and Lows*

Going on to the rocks

- *The Eurovision Song Contest is back tonight. And Gary Leboff is in despair*

Great white hope: Scott Fitzgerald, singing for Britain

● Johnny Logan

MANKIND'S morbid fascination with natural disaster will tonight persuade 400 million viewers across Europe to tune in to the Eurovision Song Contest. Conceived in 1956 as a method of promoting "peace and harmony" throughout Europe, the contest has matured into the musical equivalent of "Miss World", but with fewer pairs of shapely legs.

However, behind the impressive viewing figures, the Eurovision Song Contest is living on borrowed time. Last year Gideon Patt, the Israeli Minister Of Culture, tried to ban his country's entry as "an insult to our national intelligence". This was less serious than France's withdrawal in 1982, dismissing the contest as "a monument to drivel and mediocrity", but the writing was on the wall.

Had Britain supported an Italian boycott two years later, the fate of Eurovision would surely have been sealed. Italy and France have subsequently returned, but should BBC viewing figures continue to fall (from a late '60s peak of 20 million to 10 million last year) the future of Eurovision will again be in jeopardy.

Riding the wave of '60s fervour, the contest grew from modest origins into a forum with influence across the record industry. Lulu, Sandie Shaw and Cliff Richard were among established stars chosen to represent Great Britain, while Abba's victory with "Waterloo" in 1974 catapulted them to international stardom. However, Johnny Logan, Irish singer and double Eurovision winner (1980 and '87), feels that Abba's win began a serious decline.

" 'Waterloo' defined the song-writing formula for winning the contest," he says. "From then on all efforts at original thought were replaced by unsubtle impersonation. Then came the rule change in 1985 stipulating that all contestants sing in their native tongue — it's that bright idea we have to thank for the stream of 'A Ba Ni Bi's, 'Ding-a-dong's and 'Bang-a-bong's."

As this year's contest takes place in Dublin, and in the vain attempt to modernise Eurovision's image, the European Broadcasting Union (EBU) invited U2 to record a special video. Not surprisingly Bono and Co turned them down. "Frankly, this invitation completely missed the point," says Logan. "Only by the organisers addressing their minds to the embarrassingly low standards of songs can the contest be saved."

In an attempt to revive interest, "Top of the Pops" this year broke its own ban on records outside the Top 40 and devoted three minutes of precious air time to Britain's entry, "Go" by Scott Fitzgerald. This did not appear to register in the public consciousness: "Go" peaked at No 88 in the Gallup chart.

At Fitzgerald's record company, PRT, managing director Kim Richards blames the decline of British interest firmly on Radio One:"From the moment 'Go' was excluded from the Radio One playlist it had no chance whatsoever of becoming a hit.

"There is a complete misunderstanding of the *raison d'être* of the contest, which is the promotion of song writing. Any neutral would agree the current British charts are full of worse songs than 'Go' and if most of the Top 30 were in tonight's contest, they'd be lucky to come last."

Johnny Logan explains the reluctance of household names to take part. "Why should Boy George or Rick Astley put their careers in the hands of a jury, totally unqualified to judge their work? The only contest of relevance to them is the Top 40."

Standards could be improved by introducing a preliminary round to eliminate weaker contestants and abolishing the three-minute maximum song length. Neither, however, is acceptable to the EBU, whose prime concern remains selling the programme to all participating nations.

Battered by aesthetes and record-buyers alike, the Eurovision Song Contest does at least serve one purpose. It proves beyond reasonable doubt that 400 million people really can be wrong.

● *The contest is on BBC1, 8pm*

The Daily Telegraph, April 30th, 1988

It's no Go in Europe

BRITISH singer Scott Fitzgerald lost the Eurovision Song Contest in Dublin last night — by a single point. Scott's song Go was beaten by the Swiss entry when Britain got no marks at all from Yugoslavia, the final country to vote. BBC commentator Terry Wogan said: "This is the closest finish I've ever seen, one heartbreaking point."

Sunday Mirror, 1st May, 1988

1988

Scott Fitzgerald

After Johnny Logan's record breaking second win, the 33rd edition of Eurovision was held in Ireland at Dublin's RDS Simmonscourt on 30th April.

A total of twenty-one countries took part, there were initially twenty-two but Cyprus was disqualified for a breach of the contest's rules. The song they had opted to represent them had been published a few years earlier which was composed to represent them in a prior edition of the contest.

The winning country was Switzerland with a song titled *Ne partez pas sans moi* performed by Canadian singer Céline Dion, with 137 points, this victory helped launch Céline Dion to international stardom leading her to become one of the best-sellling artists of all time. Switzerland beat the UK entry by just one point on the final jury.

The UK entry was chosen in the usual manner through the *Song for Europe final*, the winning song was *Go* performed by Scottish singer and actor Scott Fitzgerald. He had achieved UK chart success in the 70s, he was now also the first ever winner of the UK *Song for Europe* to be chosen by the telephone vote.

The song was written by Julie Forsyth, the daughter of the entertainer Bruce Forsyth. It was later reported that Bruce was apparently annoyed that the Dutch jury had not given the UK any votes, as he had been recently working there.

The song is a ballad which tells the story of two ex-lovers bumping into each other again by chance.

The entry did extremely well, second place was no disgrace with 136 points and this was the best the UK had done since Bucks Fizz won in 1981.

The song reached number fifty-two in the UK singles charts.

Author's Comment:
No disgrace losing out to Céline Dion.

The UK in Eurovision - *The Highs and Lows*

Eurovision song time once again

Paisley Daily Express, May 6th, 1989

★ THE EUROVISION SONG CONTEST (BBC1, 8pm): Switzerland celebrates the 33rd Eurovision Song Contest — their first victory since 1956, the year it all began — by hosing the 34th. And live from Lausanne, Terry Wogan adds his own brand of humour as he guides British viewers through the annual event.

Of the 30 members of the European Broadcasting Union eligible to take part 22 are exercising their vocal chords in preparation for the major song contest in the Western World.

For the winner it often means instant stardom, as demonstrated by Swedish gorup ABBA, in 1974.

British hopes this year lie with Live Report, voted to victory by more than 100,000 viewers last month in "A Song For Europe". Maltese-born lead singer Ray Caruana and fellow group members sing "Why Do I Always Get It Wrong" by writer / composers Brian Hodgson and John Beeby.

European taster for Ray

Ray Caruana (above), the lead singer of the group Live Report, will be singing for Britain in Switzerland on May 6. And today he gets a chance to see what he will be up against when the first 11 countries perform their songs in the first part of the **Eurovision Song Contest Preview** (BBC1, 4.45pm). Among them will be Luxembourg, who have won the contest five times, and Turkey, who have failed to make any impact since they first entered in the 1970s. The second 11 will perform their songs next Sunday

Huddersfield Daily Examiner, April 22nd, 1989

1989

Live Report

After Celine Dion's narrow victory the previous year the city of Lausanne, and the Palais de Beaulieu, Switzerland held the 34th Eurovision on Saturday, 6th May. Twenty-two countries taking part with Cyprus returning after their disqualification the previous year.

Yugoslavia were the victors with a song called *Rock Me* by Croatian band Riva, this was the sole victory for Yugoslavia before the country broke up.

As of 2022 they are still the last act to win after performing last in the final.

Why Do I Always Get it Wrong? performed by Live Report was the winner of the UK *A Song for Europe* final and represented the UK in Lausanne. The band members Ray Caruana, John Beeby, Brian Hodgson, Maggie Jay, Mike Bell and Peter May came second in the Eurovision final with 130 points, only seven points behind the winners Yugoslavia. The song actually received the most twelve point awards, but it still wasn't enough to win.

The song was a ballad about a man who runs away from his lover where they won't find him, it was the only way to stop the pain. The song was written by two members of the band Brian Hodgson and John Beeby.

Allegedly Ray Caruana was a little upset about coming second to what he considered a much less worthy song.

The ballad was released as a single but only made it to number seventy-three in the UK singles chart.

Author's Comment:
Good effort, not sure why Ray was upset though, have a listen to the winning song and Live Report, you make your mind up.

*The 80s what can you say,
not the most fruitful of decades,
one absolute classic of a win in 1981
and a couple of second places, the rest
mainly forgettable.*

The 90s
1990-1999

The UK in Eurovision - *The Highs and Lows*

Euro hope for Emma

BRITAIN'S youngest Eurovision song contestant was today facing up to the challenge of attempting to bring back the title for the first time since Bucks Fizz won in 1983.

Schoolgirl Emma Booth, 15, has her fingers crossed that the song *Give a Little Love Back to the World* will launch her on a showbusiness career and put her into the pop music charts. She is the UK entrant for tomorrow's contest in Yugoslavia.

Evening Post, May 4th, 1990

1990

Emma

This was the first time the Eurovision Contest would be held in the Balkans as well as the first and only contest held in a communist state, that being Zagreb, SR Croatia, Yugoslavia at the Vatroslav Lisinski Concert Hall on 5th May.

Twenty-two countries took part, same as the previous year.

The winning country was Italy with the song *Insieme: 1992* performed by Toto Cutugno. Cutugno was the oldest winner of the contest up until the year 2000. Also worth mentioning was that this was the last time that the five countries that would become known as the 'Big Five' - Italy, France, Spain, Germany and the UK would all be placed in the top 10.

The UK was represented by Welsh singer Emma with song titled *Give A Little Love Back to the World*, the meaning of the song was about environmentalism. The song was written by Paul Curtis.

Emma had won the right to represent the UK in the usual *A Song for Europe* final on 30th March. Emma, full name Emma Louise Booth was the youngest ever entrant on behalf of the UK at the age of 15, only just being able to take part as the rules stipulate you must be 16 in the year you participate, she finished in sixth place in the final with 87 points.

After release as a single it reached thirty-three in the UK charts, highest charting Eurovision entry since 1984.

She only ever made one more record, that was the following year, but it failed to chart.

Author's Comment:
Not the greatest of starts to the new decade, but reasonable performance by Emma.

The UK in Eurovision - *The Highs and Lows*

Trinity Mirror / Mirrorpix / Alamy Stock Photo

The 90s

1991

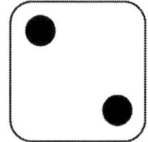

Samantha Janus

Italy, Rome and the Studio 15 di Cinecittà on the 4th May was the venue and date for the 36th Song Contest.

This wasn't the original chosen venue. Teatro Ariston in Sanremo, where the Sanremo music festival takes place yearly was going to host the competition as this was where the whole idea of the Eurovision was inspired from and the organisers thought this would be a good way of paying tribute to that idea.

Due to the Gulf war breaking out the organisers thought security would be better in the capital, so it was moved.

Twenty-two countries took part with Malta re-joining for the first time since 1975. The Netherlands opted out due to it conflicting with its national remembrance day. This was also the last time the Socialist Federal Republic of Yugoslavia participated due to the splitting up of the country after the Balkans war. Also to note was that Germany was represented in their United form after East Germany joined the West due to the German reunification.

Nearly the whole contest was hosted in Italian, which is not an official language of the European Broadcasting Union, English and French are, and it is usually mandatory to present in at least one of those languages.

Whilst we are on about the language of the presentation, this was also the last time the official logo was in a language other than English. Since 1992 the official logo has been in English.

The winner was Sweden with *Fångad av en stormvind* performed by the popular Carola. This wasn't an outright win, Sweden was tied with France's *C'est le dernier qui a parlé qui a raison* by Amina, both songs had received 146 points, so the tie-break measure was used (this was introduced in 1969 after the four-way tie). Both countries had received the same number of twelve points, but Sweden had received more ten points, so Carola was declared the winner.

The UK's *A Song for Europe* final was held on 29th March and Samantha Janus won with a song titled *A Message to Your Heart* written by Paul Curtis. The song was about the disadvantaged, the suffering from poverty and starvation.

Janus was joined by three backing singers Zoe Picot, Lucy Moorby and Nikki Belsher, their were also two other backing singers hidden, Kit Rolfe (competed for the UK in 1984) and Hazell Dean.

In the final Janus finished in tenth place with forty-seven points, this was the worst showing since 1987. Due to this the UK's selection show would be changed for 1992.

Critics slammed the performance and appearance. They thought she was dressed inappropriately in a pink mini-dress and her backing singers in white mini-dresses, considering that the theme of the song was about poverty and hardship.

The single release reached thirty in the UK singles chart. The one and only hit Samantha would have.

However Janus (now Womack) has gone on to be a successful actress, appearing in many sitcoms and of course more famously appearing in Eastenders.

Author's Comment:
Not sure she deserved the criticism for her appearance, the song yes, but at the end of the day it's show business.

1992

Michael Ball

Malmö Isstadion, Malmö, Sweden held the 37th edition of the song contest on 9th May, with twenty-three countries participating with the Netherlands returning. This set the record for countries in the history of Eurovision up to this date. This would shortly be broken again. The Federal Republic of Yugoslavia made it's last appearance as they were banned a few weeks later due to the Balkan war. This wasn't the Socialist Federal Republic of Yugoslavia which we mentioned in the 1991 text, this was in fact Serbia and Montenegro (known as the Federal Republic of Yugoslavia).

The competition was won by Ireland's Linda Martin, who previously came in second place in 1984, and of course Johnny Logan had to be involved somewhere, he wrote the song.

Linda Martin remains to this day the oldest woman ever to win Eurovision at the age of 41.

A fact worth bringing to your attention, the UK finished second with Malta third, this was the first time the top three placed songs were all sung in English.

Now the UK representative, due to the disappointment of the previous year's entry, *A Song for Europe* was changed, the multi-artist format which had been used from 1976 to 1991 was dropped in favour of the format used from 1964 to 1975, one artist performing all the songs.

The chosen artist this year was singer, presenter and actor Michael Ball, already a successful star on the West End and had a hit UK single with *Love Changes Everything*.

The final took place on 3rd April and the winning song was *One Step Out of Time* written by Paul Davies, Tony Ryan and Victor Stratton.

The theme of the song is about the singer's comfort with being "one step out of time" in relation to the reality around him, instead

The UK in Eurovision - *The Highs and Lows*

pining after his former lover. The mid-tempo ballad finished as we mentioned earlier in second place with 139 points. Despite the loss to Ireland the UK entry in fact achieved more twelve points than the Irish entry.

The song reached a respectable 20th place in the UK singles chart.

Worth mentioning was he was awarded the Order of the British Empire Medal in the Queen's Birthday honours list of 2015 his services to musical theatre.

Author's Comment:
I really believe the performance and song was worthy of winning.

Liverpool Echo, April 3rd, 1992

1993

Sonia

Ireland, Millstreet and the Green Glens Arena on 15th May hosted the 38th Eurovision final.

Millstreet is the smallest town ever to hold the Eurovision final with a population of only 1500 people.

A new record of twenty-five countries took part, with the breaking up of the former republic of Yugoslavia many new countries wanted to take part, therefore Bosnia and Herzegovina, Croatia and Slovenia all competed for the first time.

Ireland won for the second year running with *In Your Eyes* by Niamh Kavanagh. This was Ireland's fifth victory which equalled France and Luxembourg. Ireland also became the fourth country to win for the second time in a row, also by chance the top two countries this year were the same as the previous year with the UK second.

As per the previous year one artist was chosen for the UK to perform eight songs for *A Song for Europe* final on 9th April. The chosen artist was Sonia, full name Sonia Evans and the winning song was *Better the Devil You Know* written by Dean Collinson and Brian Teasdale.

Sonia was already a successful artist before Eurovision with eleven top UK hits between 1989 and 1993. She was the first female artist to achieve five hit singles from one album.

Better the Devil You Know had a retro Rock 'n' Roll sound and the song tells the story of how in love she is with her boyfriend and she would sell her heart and soul to get his unconditional love.

The second place finish at the final in Ireland was the UK's fourth second place since 1988 and 14th overall.

The single reached number 15 on the UK singles chart and stayed in the chart for seven weeks.

She has since appeared in musicals in the West End and released several albums.

The UK in Eurovision - *The Highs and Lows*

*Author's Comment:
Great performance,
should have won!*

● In tune... British songstress Sonia practises her song for Europe, Better the Devil You Know, before tonight's exciting final between 25 countries in Cork, Ireland

SONIA and TERRY WOGAN at Eurovision Song Contest... BBC1 at 8 pm

Eastern Europeans add to sound of Eurovision music

Sonia will have to be on song for the final round of the *Eurovision Song Contest.*

Britain's hope will join a willing band which this year includes seven of the newest members of the European Broadcasting Union — from eastern Europe.

The qualifiers were Bosnia herzegovina, Croatia and Slovenia and they join 22 countries to make a record entry of 29.

Sonia will sing Dean Collinson and Red's (Brian Teasdale) *Better The Devil You Know* and adding to the hype will be Terry Wogan with his particular brand of comment, opinion and wit — for the 13th consecutive year, by the way.

The UK last won the contest when Bucks Fizz sang *Making Up Your Mind Up* in 1982. (BBC1 8 pm).

Ayreshire Post, May 14th, 1993

SONIA IS ON SONG FOR EURO CONTEST

Family wait at home and hope for a British win

By Will Rolston

SINGING star Sonia's family were braced for some Eurovision excitement today.

The 90-strong Evans clan were keeping their fingers crossed that Sonia's British entry will scoop top prize in tonight's song contest.

Most nervous were Sonia's parents Danny and Pat Evans.

The couple, from St David's Road, Birkenhead, will be on the edge of their seats, when daughter Sonia takes to the Eurovision stage.

"We are very, very excited. It is a fantastic honour for us all," Pat told the ECHO today.

Powerful

The couple would have loved to be at the 25-nation contest near Cork in Ireland but say "personal reasons" forced them to stay at home and watch the drama unfold courtesy of the BBC.

Family backing of the most powerful kind comes from Carol, Sonia's 29-year-old sister, who will be on stage behind her sister singing her heart out for Europe.

Sonia wants to be first to win for Britain since Bucks Fizz swept the board in 1981.

And she has expressed her admiration for other star winners Lulu and Cliff Richard.

She said: "I used to love watching the contest as a kid. Bucks Fizz were my favourite.

Liverpool Echo, May 15th, 1993

"I was ten when they won, so it's about time we won again."

The singer's granny, Kate Evans, 83, a former professional singer, is having a party at her flat in Kirkdale.

She said: "We've been praying for her every night. It's a real honour and we've all got our fingers crossed."

Terry Wogan last week gave Sonia's song Better The Devil You Know "nil points" in his personal assessment of the British entry.

But Kate and the rest of the family are sure she will win.

1994

Francis Ruffelle

Back in Ireland again after winning again in 1993, but this time we are back in Dublin, at the Point Theatre on 30th April.

Twenty-five countries took part equalling the previous year's record, a total of seven countries took part for the first time, Estonia, Hungary, Lithuania, Poland, Romania, Russia and Slovakia. To cope with this increase in countries wishing to compete in the Song contest governing body ruled that the seven lowest placed countries from 1993 couldn't participate. So that meant Belgium, Cyprus, Denmark, Israel, Luxembourg, Slovenia and Turkey were relegated, but due to the withdrawal of Italy, Cyprus was reinstated. Luxembourg has never participated ever again.

Unbelievably Ireland won for the third time in a row with *Rock 'n' Roll Kids* performed by Paul Harrington and Charlie McGettigan.

This is the first time in the history of the contest that a country had won three in a row and it also made Ireland the country with the most wins in Eurovision history with six victories.

For the first time voting was done by Satellite not telephone, this also enabled viewers to see the juries deliver the results.

Same as the previous year the BBC announced a sole candidate to sing a selection of songs for the UK entry, the chosen artist this time was musical theatre actress and singer Frances Ruffelle. She had won a Tony award in 1987 and was thought to be a solid choice for Eurovision.

The winning song voted for on the 18th March in the *Song for Europe* final was *Lonely Symphony* written by George De Angelis and Mark Dean. The song was an atmospheric gospel song, not the usual for a Eurovision entry. The critic for *Smash Hits* magazine at the time quoted, "Everyone makes jokes about the Eurovision Song Contest, but we all want to win. Frances Ruffelle is a rather wonderful, gutsy singer who could sing the London phone directory and make it sound good. And guess what? She just has!"

Unfortunately it wasn't good enough and she finished down the leader board in tenth place with a haul of sixty-three points.

It did make number twenty-five in the singles charts.

Author's Comment:
The song was too unusual to win Eurovision, but it if you listen a few times it does grow on you.

1995

Love City Groove

Back in Dublin again for the 40th Eurovision, also back at the Point Theatre on the 13th May.

Twenty-three countries took part with Estonia, Finland, Lithuania, Romania, Slovakia, Switzerland and the Netherlands being relegated to allow Belgium, Denmark, Israel, Slovenia and Turkey back after being relegated after the 1993 final.

Norway ran out winners this year with the song *Nocturne* performed by Secret Garden. Funnily enough their was an Irish connection with the Norwegian winners Secret Garden, the violinist Fionnuala Sherry was Irish.

Worth noting was this was the first winner that was mainly instrumental with the song containing a total of only twenty-four words, with brief vocals at the start and at the end of the performance.

Due to the disappointing result the previous year the *Song for Europe* UK final went back to the format last used in 1991 where different acts performed again. At the final on 31st March, Love City Groove won with the song *Love City Groove* written and performed by Stephen Rudden, Tatsiana Mais, Jay Williams and Paul Hardy.

Love City Grove were a rap group and the entry of the same name was an upbeat reggae pop track.

Journalist from Music Week's *RM Dance Update* wrote, "A very pleasant mid-tempo groove with great vocals and a bit of rapping that swings along beautifully in quite old-fashioned jazz funk way and it really gets on your brain. Only trouble is it's a real summer tune.

Once again a disappointing result followed in the final, finishing the same as the previous year in tenth place with a points tally of seventy-six.

The UK public seemed to the like the song though as the single released faired better with a peak of number seven in the UK singles charts with over 200,000 in sales.

The UK in Eurovision - *The Highs and Lows*

Get into the Groove!

Eurovision SPECIAL

The UK's contender in tonight's Eurovision Song Contest is threatening to turn the competition upside down. **Mark Barden** gets the lowdown on Love City Groove.

Star Chat

When Love City Groove were asked to enter this year's Song For Europe, their reaction could have been understood in any language. To put it mildly, they weren't keen. It took all the persuasive powers of competition supremo Jonathan King to get the group to change their minds, and even then they agreed more out of their collective sense of fun – albeit with one eye, admits LCG's creator Beanz, on the useful publicity.

King was determined to make sure that the UK's 1995 Eurovision contender's sound was fresh and different, and as far as the British public were concerned nothing sounded as fresh and different as the infectiously hip 'Love City Groove'. In the face of seemingly stiff competition, Beanz and his slightly bemused team won the Song For Europe phone poll by a landslide.

"We thought the idea of us in The Eurovision Song Contest was crazy," smiles Beanz (28) before a photo shoot in a basement studio off London's Kings Road. "But when we said 'no' Jonathan asked us to think again and gradually managed to convince us that this year's Song For Europe was going to be different, with good writers and good bands. He wanted us to be part of making it credible, and we also realised it would guarantee us a lot of exposure, so it started to seem like a wise move. But it was such a shock when we actually won."

No-one was more shocked than rapper Reason. She joined Beanz, Jay Williams and Paul Hardy in Love City Groove just two weeks before the competition after the departure of another female rap artist. "When they first mentioned Song For Europe I said 'No way, I'm not doing it'. The guys finally persuaded me it could be a good thing but I still went 'undercover' by wearing dark glasses and having my hair down! I definitely didn't think we'd win and when we did I was just screaming 'Oh no!'. I still wasn't looking at the thing in a positive way but when I saw how many votes we'd won by I realised a lot of people must be into rap, anyway."

"We definitely approached it with a kind of tongue-in-cheek attitude," says Paul (26), who co-fronts LCG with Reason and provides the group's more soulful vibes. "But the song is so strong and so different to what's gone on before that it's really taken off. It wasn't written as a 'Eurovision' song and it's nothing like the typical jingly, poppy number or ballad that people think they have to come up with."

According to LCG's youngest member, Jay (21), The Eurovision Song Contest needs to head in the direction the group hope to take it at Dublin's Point Theatre on Saturday May 13. "It's got a naff image but it shouldn't have," says the basketball-loving rapper and club DJ. "The contest should be a shop window for new talent but unfortunately it's become a bit set in its ways. It hasn't moved with the times and young people especially treat it as a bit of a joke. We want to help change that, and whether we win or lose we'll stand out because we're so different."

"We could be part of something that gives the whole thing a kick up the 90s," agrees Paul, who's sung with Sade and Tom Jones and is about to work with Dina Carroll. "If things change in this country they might start to change abroad, too, and not before time. If that happens then we'll have done our job. If not then I don't think Eurovision will survive.

"Some people have said they're not ready for our kind of sound in Europe, but in my experience people on the continent are really into hip-hop, rap or dance with English lyrics so I don't think we'll sound too alien to them."

If British reactions are anything to go by, 'Love City Groove' – already a chart success – will be the people's choice, whatever the Eurovision judges decide. "The reaction has been amazing," confirms Beanz, LCG's producer and main writer who's looking forward to becoming a dad in June. "We've been doing roadshows round the country and when that chorus kicks in and you have a couple of thousand voices singing 'In the morning..... we can't hear ourselves. It's fantastic."

Hull Daily Mail, May 13th, 1995

Author's Comment:
Good tune, the song would probably do better in present day Eurovision!

1996

Gina G

The 41st song contest was held at the Oslo Spektrum in Oslo, Norway on the 18th May.

Thirty countries submitted entries, the usual relegation system was changed this year with a secret audio-only qualifying round held two months prior to the final to reduce the number of participants to twenty-two countries. This didn't include the host nation. The countries eliminated from this round were Denmark, Germany, Hungary, Israel, Macedonia, Romania and Russia. This was the first time Germany were absent from the start of Eurovision in 1956.

The winner once again was Ireland, their record breaking seventh win and fourth win in five years with *The Voice* performed by Eimear Quinn.

A note worth mentioning, this was the final time all the results were determined solely by jury voting.

The UK entry was chosen from a new show *The Great British Song Contest 1996*, it consisted of a semi-final and a final both broadcast by the BBC. Eight songs by eight different artists were played on March 1st on a special edition of *Top of the Pops* and the four songs with the highest telephone votes went through to the final on March 8th.

The winner with the highest votes was Gina G with *Ooh Aah... Just a Little Bit*. Gina G is an Australian singer songwriter and this was her debut solo single. The song was written by Simon Caldwell and Steve Rodway.

The rules in 1996 required that all the instruments used on the backing track for the song must be represented on stage. Due to the fact that the song was made up of mostly computer generated sounds a couple of Apple mac computers were placed on stage beside two synthesizers.

The critics seemed to respond well to the song and one newspaper the Scottish *Aberdeen Evening Post* described the song as a slice of

The UK in Eurovision - *The Highs and Lows*

cheesy Europop. You will either love it or hate it. Swedish newspaper *Expressen* called it "sticky yummy pop pastry".

Disappointingly she finished in eighth place in the final with seventy-seven points.

The song was a massive hit in the UK charts reaching number one and reached high chart positions all over Europe and even in the USA which was a rarity for a Eurovision release. It reached number twelve on the Billboard top 100, and it was even nominated at the Grammy Awards in 1998 for best Dance Recording.

In 2012 it was ranked at number 45 in NME's list of the 50 best-selling tracks of the 90s, selling in excess of 790,000 copies.

Evening Post, May 18th, 1996

Author's Comment:
Fantastic Eurovision entry, and what a performance from Gina.

The 90s

The UK in Eurovision - *The Highs and Lows*

1997

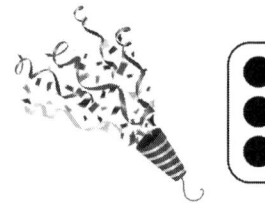 

Katrina and the Waves

The 42nd Eurovision was held in Dublin, Ireland at the Point Theatre on 3rd May.

Twenty-five countries participated. A new relegation system was introduced for determining which countries could participate. This time each country's average points total in previous contests was calculated. Italy made its first appearance since 1993, and Denmark, Germany, Hungary and Russia returned after last competing in 1995. Belgium, Finland and Slovakia, participants in the previous year's contest, were unable to return after being excluded by the new rules. Before we go onto the winner and the UK entry a new system of voting was trialled at this event, five countries used televoting to determine their points allocated. This allowed the public a say in the outcome for the first time. Following the success of this trial, all countries were encouraged to adopt the same system of voting from 1998 onwards.

Also for the first time no live music accompaniment was needed, with each song being able to use a backing track rather than any part of an orchestra or live instruments the performers might use.

Now the winner this year was the UK with *Love Shine a Light* by Katrina and the Waves, and the members of the group was made up of Canadian national Katrina Leskanich, Kimberley Rew, Vince de la Cruz, Alex Cooper and Miriam Stockley.

They were already a successful rock group with one massive hit behind them, *Walking On Sunshine* in the mid eighties.

Love Shine a Light had won through the usual UK's Great British Song Contest 1997 semi-final and final to represent the UK.

The song had been composed by the group's guitarist and regular songwriter Kimberley Rew. It was originally going to be used for an anthem for Samaritans in recognition of the thirtieth anniversary of the Swindon branch of the organisation, but it was the members of that group that made the comment that the song was the type of song that should represent the UK in Eurovision and could possibly win it. So it was entered.

Kimberley Rew the guitarist and composer didn't perform with the band at the UK event or the Eurovision final in Dublin, he did accompany Katrina for the congratulations on stage at the UK event. But didn't really want anything to do with the dream of winning the Eurovision.

The song was the bookmakers favourite going into the final and it didn't disappoint. *Love Shine a Light* won the contest easily with a points tally of 227. It was given ten sets of maximum twelve points.

The song received an average of 9.458 points per country or 78.82% of total votes available, the third-highest in the history of the present voting system.

It became a big hit all over Europe and peaked at number three in the UK singles chart.

One note of mention was that 1997 was the first time an openly LBGT artist was selected to represent a country in the final. That being Paul Oscar for Iceland.

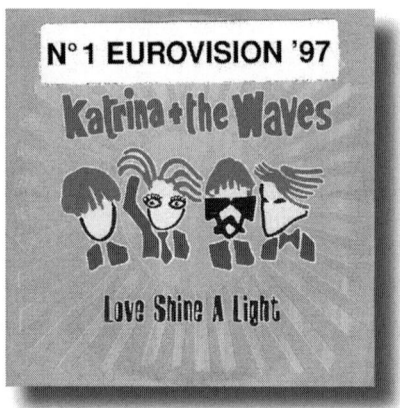

Author's Comment:
The Samaritans certainly know a winner, and what a winner, one of the all time classic Eurovision anthems!

The 90s

Boom Bang a Bang

Watch out! It's Eurovision Song Contest time again

THE Eurovision Song Contest is here again. The time of year when a motley collection of music from all over the Continent clashes head-on to see which one strikes a chord with a majority of the judges. Britain, says TIM DAVEY, has high hopes — again!

LOVE shine a light in every corner of my heart ... light up the magic in every little part ... remember the words well, by tomorrow all of Europe could be singing or humming them.

For, if both Terry Wogan and chart-topping popster Jonathan King are to be believed, these are the lyrics which could see us crowned champions of Europe in the vocal league.

Both men's views are worth respecting. Terry in particular has seen more than his fair share of *Eurovision Song Contest* (Tonight, BBC1, 8pm) action.

And they reckon *Love Shine A Light*, the British entry sung by Katrina And The Waves, has the best chance in years of ensuring United Kingdom glory in the continent-wide contest.

For the first time ever the vast audience is being given a chance to have a say on who should win.

● There are 25 countries taking part this year. Onet eliminated since last year are Belgium, Finland, Lithuania, Luxembourg, Romania and Slovakia.
● This contest has been running since 1956 and the UK entered for the first time in 1957. Patricia Bredin sang a song called A8. We didn't enter the following year!
● UK songs have won four times: Sandie Shaw's Puppet On A String in 1967; Lulu's Boom-Bang-A-Bang jointly in 1969; Brotherhood Of Man's Save Your Kisses For Me in 1976; and the Bucks Fizz song, Making Your Mind Up in 1981.
● Ireland tops the winners' table with seven wins.
● Johnny Logan has won THREE times. The Irish singer triumphed with What's Another Year (1980), Hold Me Now (1987) and Why Me, which he composed and saw sung by Linda Martin, in 1992.

Arrangements have been made for viewers to cast their vote by telephone.

Ireland, once again, hosts the contest live from the Point Theatre in Dublin. The show features a top of the bill appearance by pop phenomenon Boyzone who'll be singing to a Euro-audience of 300 million and a worldwide audience of twice that figure.

Terry Wogan is definitely backing Katrina And The Waves: "It's our best chance to win since Bucks Fizz in 1981. They will score better than anybody for the UK since Michael Ball came second five years ago."

Though, as if hedging his bet, he then adds: "Our entry needs to be twice as good as anybody else's to win. Remember the UK is easily the most unpopular country in Europe."

Jonathan King, music executive in charge of our entry selection, reckons Katrina and Co's song is "one of the most catchy, anthemic, singalong, pop records in years and a dead cert to win."

Katrina herself is just proud to be given the chance to sing for Britain: "I can't think of it as a greater honour than to represent the country I love and have lived in for more than 20 years."

Her group has already tasted success. Back in 1985 their summertime hit *Walking On Sunshine* hit the charts. This song, written by group member Kimberley Rew, was actually penned for the Samaritans' 30th anniversary but the band decided to make it a Euro entry at the last minute.

The contest has now been running for 42 years.

Britain, along with Austria, Sweden, Switzerland and Germany, has introduced a telephone voting system to help decide the final outcome.

The phone lines will open once all 25% songs have been performed at a maximum calls cost of 10p

BUT, just like the official judging panels, voters will NOT be allowed to choose their own country, so no UK votes can go to Katrina.

Ronan Keating, a member of Ireland's chart group Boyzone, will help host proceedings and perform a new song he wrote specially for the occasion as part of an interval dance and music extravaganza.

Terry Wogan reckons the group's appearance confirms that Eurovision, always scoffed at over here, has now become trendy.

"It has always been huge in Europe. It took a while for the penny to drop in the UK.

"Now even the most blase are at least pretending to get the joke.

"The Europeans have always taken it with deadly seriousness.

"It is to Britain's eternal credit that the public here have regarded it as grandiose silliness from the beginning."

Terry, of course, plays his part in keeping that over-view alive and kicking with his off-screen comments on the night's three-hour proceedings.

● MY SHOUT: Lulu after winning the contest (above). Bucks Fizz (above left) went from strength to strength

Evening Post, May 3rd, 1997

1998

Imaani

43rd Eurovision was held in Birmingham, UK at the National Indoor Arena on 9th May.

Twenty-five countries took part, Austria, Bosnia and Herzegovina, Denmark, Iceland and Russia dropped out this year due to lowest average points total over their previous five contests, Italy chose not to participate. Macedonia made its first appearance, Belgium, Finland, Israel, Romania and Slovakia made a return.

Winning country was Israel with the song *Diva* performed by Dana International. Dana International was the first transgender participant and the contests first openly LGBTQ+ winning artist.

The participation of Dana International caused widespread condemnation in sections of Israeli society and there were death threats against her in the run-up to the competition.

It was also the first contest where televoting predominated.

The UK entry was picked once again through *The Great British Song Contest 1998* a semi-final and a final, the usual eight songs sung by eight artists, top four going through to the final on 15th March.

Imaani full name Imaani Saleem came out winner with a song called *Where Are You*, written by Scott English, Phil Maniukiza and Simon Stirling.

The song was a regarded as a dark, thumping house track, and is regarded as one of the UK's better Eurovision entries, finishing in second place with 166 points, 15th time the UK had finished second. But this was the last time the UK came within a chance of winning, that is until last year 2022.

The song achieved widespread success in many countries becoming a top twenty hit throughout Europe and peaked within the top ten in the UK singles charts.

It was included on the popular music compilation album for 1998, *Now That's What I Call Music! 40*.

The 90s

This was Imaani's only ever solo hit.

In 2017 the official website for the Eurovision Song Contest ranked *Where Are You* at number six on their list of all time best UK Eurovision entries. A worthy Legacy to a good song.

Birmingham Evening Mail, May 5th, 1998

Author's Comment:
Stonking good entry, it should have done better, deserved first place.

The UK in Eurovision - *The Highs and Lows*

1999

Precious

The last Eurovision Song Contest of the twentieth century, the 44th, was held on 29th May at the International Convention Centre in Jerusalem, Israel.

The staging of the competition in Jerusalem wasn't without its objectors. The Orthodox Jewish Community and the deputy mayor were just a cross section of people of objected.

Twenty-three countries took part with the usual relegations, this time Finland, Greece, Hungary, Macedonia, Romania, Slovakia and Switzerland, with Austria, Bosnia and Herzegovina, Denmark and Iceland returning and Lithuania making a welcome return, last seen in 1994.

A new relegation rule was going to be introduced in 2000 and future contests — the four largest financial contributors to the competition, namely Germany, UK, France and Spain would be exempt from relegation. This group of nations now known as the *Big Four* was to ensure the financial viability of the event was always sustained. As the results of these four countries were not always that good it therefore stopped any worry that they would be relegated, resulting in a hole in the funding.

So the *Big Four* was born.

This year's winning entry was Sweden's *Take Me to Your Heaven* performed by Charlotte Nilsson. This was Sweden's fourth success.

The UK entry came through the usual channels that is to say *The Great British Song Contest 1999* and the girl group Precious was chosen with a song titled *Say It Again* written by Paul Varney.

The group consisted of members Louise Rose, Anya Lahiri, Kalli Clark-Stemberg, Jenny Frost and Sophie McDonnell.

They performed fifth at the final but came a disappointing twelfth place with only thirty-eight points, the worst showing for quite a while for the UK. In fact the first time since 1987 that the UK finished

The 90s

outside the top ten.

It faired better in the UK singles charts peaking at number six.

The group did go on to put out more material and had some limited success before finally disbanding in 2001. Jenny Frost went on to be a member of the British girl supergroup Atomic Kitten and Sophie McDonnell went onto become a TV host. Louise Rose moved into acting and Kali Clark-Sternberg found work as a session singer whilst Anya Lahiri returned to modelling and acting.

Author's Comment:
A disappointing end to the century!

Evening Post, 29th May, 1999

The UK in Eurovision - *The Highs and Lows*

*The 90s was a bit of a hit and miss decade with
one massive win and three second places,
the others left sadly wanting and
rather than leaving the century with a bang,
we went out with a whimper!*

The 2000s
2000-2009

2000

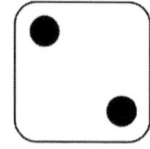

Nikki French

The start of a new century for Eurovision and the first final of the 21st century is at the Globe Arena, Stockholm, Sweden on the 13th May.

Twenty-four countries took part, Latvia taking part for the first time, Slovakia, Hungary and Greece decided against participating due to financial reasons. Finland, Macedonia, Romania and Switzerland returned, Russia also made a comeback, Bosnia and Herzegovina, Lithuania, Portugal, Poland and Slovenia were relegated. This year also marked the first year the *Big Four* automatically qualify.

For only their second time Denmark won with the song *Fly on the Wings of Love* performed by the Olsen Brothers.

With the new Millennium the BBC decided to revert to *A Song for Europe* again for the national competition to find the performer to represent the UK. The format was the same as *The Great British Song Contest*, eight different artists performing their songs, with a semi-final and then a final. The winner this time was English singer Nikki French and *Don't Play That Song Again* written by John Springate and Gerry Shephard.

Nikki French was already quite a well-known name, she had had a world-wide hit with a remake of *Total Eclipse of the Heart* by Bonnie Tyler.

Unfortunately she probably should have taken heed to the title of her song *Don't Play That Song Again* as it came in sixteenth place in the final with a grand total of only twenty-eight points, the worst ever showing by a UK entry.

It didn't do much better either in the UK singles chart peaking at only number thirty-four, the lowest placing since 1989.

Author's Comment:
Not a great start to the new Millennium!

2001

Lindsay Dracass

The Eurovision circus moved on to Denmark, Copenhagen and the Parken Stadium for the 46th Eurovision Final on the 12th May.

Due to financial constraints there had been a problem to find a suitable venue, so the Parken Stadium was chosen, but there were complaints about the stadium being too big, with an audience of 38,000, making this the biggest venue ever to host the competition. But many of the audience couldn't see the stage and some of the acts felt it was also too big and lost some of its charm.

Twenty-three countries took part, Bosnia and Herzegovina, Lithuania, Poland, Portugal and Slovenia returned with Greece coming back after their two year sabbatical with financial difficulties. Austria, Belgium, Cyprus, Finland, Macedonia, Romania and the Swiss dropped out with relegation.

Estonia with the song *Everybody* sung by Tanel Padar, Dave Benton and 2XL and written by Ivar Must and Maian-Anna Karmas won the contest, the first time one of the countries from the former Eastern Bloc won. Worth noting Dave Benton was the first black person to win the music competition and at the age of fifty also the eldest.

The winning UK entrant was chosen through the *A Song for Europe* and the winning song *No Dream Impossible* written by Russ Ballad and Chris Winter was performed by Lindsay Dracass a 16-year-old schoolgirl.

She performed at sixteenth place in the final, but it was in fact a dream too far as the song only finished one place better than the previous year, that being fifteenth place with the same number of points twenty-eight.

It faired a little better than the previous year's entry in the UK singles charts, peaking two places higher at thirty-two.

The UK in Eurovision - *The Highs and Lows*

The setback at Eurovision didn't seem to deter Dracass as in later years she toured Europe with Paul Carrack and his band, and supported The Eagles on their 2009 tour.

Save us from the sarcasm

THE Grim Reaper is playing havoc with business at my Dangerous Liaisons Marriage Bureau. For some time, it's not been *technically* possible for Whoopi Goldberg to marry Peter Cushing and become Whoopi Cushing (on account of him being a rotting corpse), nor can Florence Griffith Joyner wed Perry Como to become Flo-Jo Como (they're *both* now wearing pine overcoats), and if George Best doesn't get his suicidal thirst under control soon, Susan George won't ever be able to tie the knot and call herself Susan George-Best. However, it *is* still possible that Isla St Clair could wed Barry White, then commit bigamy by marrying Bryan Ferry, and start calling herself Isla White-Ferry. Indeed, she could even give herself a nickname based on a weak pun: "Don't call me Isla Wight-Ferry, call me dung ... I come steaming out of the back of Cowes." Bigamy, by the way is having one husband or wife too many. Rather like monogamy.

Female singers in The **Eurovision Song Contest** (BBC1) seldom visit my bureau, probably because most of them suffer from a distressing disorder called MS (Missing Surname). Over the past 46 years, we've had the likes of Lulu, Dana, Sonia, and Anabela warbling bland, pasteurised Europop for our delectation, and Saturday night's shenanigans introduced us to a new crop of MS sufferers, including Vanna from Croatia and a pair of Michelles (one Dutch, another from Germany). Plucky contestants from 23 "European" countries (including Israel, but not one of the many Arab countries that are geographically closer) performed in Copenhagen on behalf of their various nation states, and every one made it clear from the outset that they weren't going to let lack of talent stand in the way of their careers. Yet despite the often dodgy intonation, and the frequently passé fashions and dance manoeuvres on display, there was only one truly embarrassing anachronism in evidence, and that was the BBC's commentator and "Eurovision pundit", Mr Terence Wogan.

It's long been *de rigueur* in Britain to pour scorn (of the "it's all Boom-Tinga-Linga-Bang-Bing-Bang-Bong" variety) on this annual unmusical torture-fest, but each passing year confirms that Wogan's sarcastic contribution to the event is not a soothing balm, but a noxious irritant. The man is not only as burnt-out as his jokes, but flabby to boot (I doubt if he's seen his own penis since 1971), and beneath his mock self-effacement lies a thoroughly nasty and indefensible desire to humiliate foreign broadcasters by rudely talking over them, or deliberately giving away the pay-offs to their gags (which he's seen in rehearsal, of course).

I was quite unable to discover whether or not Natasja Crone and Sören Pilmark were entertaining hosts, because their every appearance was drowned out by Wogan with leaden cries of "oh no, it's the Little Mermaid and Dr Death", "time to make the tea" or "they drain you of all emotion" like a theatre critic who gives us his opinions not in a newspaper review, but loudly from the front row of the stalls during the performance. Maybe the couple weren't overly riveting, but at least they were being unamusing in their second language. What was Wogan's excuse? I confess that the hair-hatted one's relentless xenophobia persuaded me to take an extended lavatory break just after the Russian contestant appeared ('he's not quite the full shilling", quipped our commentator), and by the time I got back, the Polish singer was doing a Buck's Fizz with her anorak, and my TV was registering 9.8 on the Wogan Eurocondescension scale.

STILL, it's his peerless knowledge of the genre that the BBC value, I suppose, and he duly informed us that the winner would be either France, Greece, or Denmark, then muttered darkly about gross voting irregularities amongst "the Baltics" when Estonia (who he had completely ignored) won by a mile. Then, displaying his detailed familiarity with the rules, he praised the UK's Lindsay Dracass for "avoiding relegation", although Eurovision regulations make it impossible for Britain ever to be relegated, no matter how badly it performs. Which is a pity because, as with *Jeux sans frontières*, it's obvious that this is a meaningless euro-event that should have been put out of our misery long ago.

It's unnatural for most of these countries to produce songs in English, but they know they'll finish nowhere if they have the effrontery to sing *"Só sei ser feliz assim"* in their native tongue, or include words like *Werkheiligkeit*, and it's always depressing to hear performers from a country like Turkey (a culture with a rich tradition of microtonal music) straightjacketing themselves into conformity with pre-packaged Eurochords I, IV, V, and VI. At times, I simply couldn't bear to look at the screen, and instead stared at the floor, so part of this column ought by rights to be devoted to a review of a cheap rug. Which brings us back, I suppose, to Terry Wogan.

Interesting article published in the Evening Standard May 14th, 2001

Author's Comment:
Rather a weird song, can see why it didn't do very well.

The 2000s

2002

Jessica Garlick

Tallin, Estonia and the Saku Suurhall hosted the 47th Eurovision final on the 25th May.

Twenty-four countries participated. Austria, Cyprus, Belgium, Finland, Macedonia, Switzerland and Romania returned whilst Iceland, Ireland, Netherlands, Norway and Poland were relegated.

Due to internal problems Portugal dropped out with Latvia replacing them. This turned out to be a stroke of luck for Latvia as they went on to win the competition with the song *I Wanna* performed by Marie N. The critics and bookmakers favourites for the competition, Denmark, ended up finishing last.

The UK's *A Song for Europe* final was won by Jessica Garlick with a song titled *Come Back* written by Martyn Baylay. The BBC had wanted a young pop singer to represent the UK and they got their wish. Garlick an English/Welsh pop singer had previously appeared on the TV talent show *Pop Idol* in 2001.

After the last couple of disastrous years it certainly was a comeback by the UK, accompanied by five backing singers she finished in third place with a total of 111 points.

The song peaked at number thirteen in the UK singles charts.

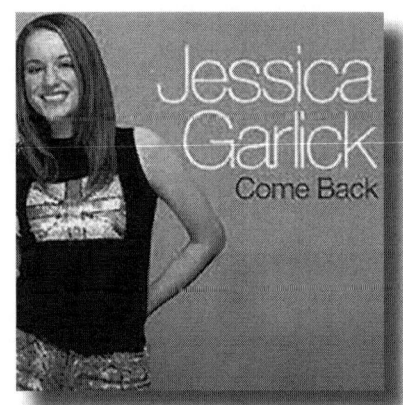

Author's Comment:
What a difference a year makes,
much better, good performance from Jessica.

2003

Jemini

The 48th edition of the competition was held in Riga, Latvia at the Skonto Hall on 24th May.

Twenty-six countries participated beating the record of twenty-five set in 1993. Iceland, Ireland, the Netherlands, Norway and Poland returned after being relegated and Portugal also returned, Ukraine made their debut, whilst Denmark, Finland, Lithuania, Macedonia and Switzerland dropped out after poor results in 2002.

Turkey recorded their first ever victory with a song titled *Everyway That I Can* performed by Sertab Erener.

A couple of points worth mentioning before we come to the UK, Latvia the host nation finished third from last. This was the worst performance from a host nation since 1992 and the first time since 1995 the host nation didn't finish in the top 10.

This was also the last contest to take place over just one evening. The EBU announced that it would be adding a semi-final show to the competition in order to accommodate the growing number of countries wishing to participate, so this was the last year that the relegation system was used to determine which countries took part in the final.

Now the UK entrant was selected through the usual channel *A Song for Europe* final and the pop duo Jemini who were Chris Cromby and Gemma Abbey with the song *Cry Baby* written by Martin Isherwood came out the winner.

The song was a simple pop song about a woman telling her lover the relationship is over. The duo were supported by three female backing singers and a guitarist for the final. Unfortunately it was a fiasco, their performance was way off key, they finished last with the distinction of being the first UK entry to have nul points!

Terry Wogan long time Eurovision commentator for the BBC

The 2000s

thought the UK was suffering from a post Iraq war backlash, but the majority of the media blamed the result on the poor quality of the song and the artists, with one critic calling the song a disgrace and deserving of last place.

In the book *The Eurovision Song Contest – The Official History* Jemini taking part in a field of twenty-six nations made the UKs null points the most spectacular in the history of the competition.

It wasn't all bad news for the duo, they did have a minor hit on their hands as the song peaked at number 15 in the UK singles charts.

Author's Comment:
I don't want to criticise too much, not sure if the nerves got to them or they really can't sing? But this was the first entry where I was embarrassed to watch. One of the biggest lows in Eurovosion for me!

DISMAL... British entry Jemini made history.

Sunday Sun, May 25th, 2003

2004

James Fox

The 49th Contest was held in Istanbul, Turkey at the Abdi ipekci Arena on 15th May.

Now the reason I have been mentioning the returning and relegations of countries in the previous years is because this has what has led us to the new format. With so many countries wishing to participate it has forced the EBU to introduce a semi-final and a final, we now see the start of a two show broadcasting. This allows all countries that want to participate to take part.

Thirty-six countries participated, beating the previous record of twenty-six the previous year. Albania, Andorra, Belarus and Serbia and Montenegro took part for the first time. All those countries that were relegated the previous year were allowed back in.

The mechanism of how this worked was that the *Big Four* went straight through to the final and the top ten countries from the 2003 contest also went straight through to the final and that left the other twenty-two countries to fight it out in the semi-final. Thereby the top ten from the semi-final went through and performed at the final.

Phew... after all of that the eventual winner was Ukraine with a song titled *Wild Dances* performed by Ruslana.

A little political point worth mentioning, this was the first year that Turkey voted for Cyprus and the second year Cyprus voted for Turkey, however this still enraged some sections of the Cypriot community.

Now the UK entry was picked through a brand new show called *Making Your Mind UP 2004*. The new format had six artists selected by Sony Music UK to compete in a final aired on TV on 28th February.

The public got to vote for their favourite and this year James Fox with a song titled *Hold Onto Our Love*, written by Gary Miller and Tim Woodcock was the winner.

James Fox real name James Richard Mullett was best known for his time on the TV talent show Fame Academy aired in 2003.

He performed with his guitar at number twenty in the final, but however much talent he had, it didn't seem to go down well with the European voters, he came a lowly sixteenth place with twenty-nine points.

It did reach number thirteen in the UK singles chart.

Fox has carried on with his musical career after Eurovision and has toured with many well known artists, Lulu, Wet Wet Wet and Tina Turner to name a few, he has also appeared in musical theatre productions.

Author's Comment:
I liked this song, it wouldn't have gone down to badly at a country music awards show. It wasn't a country song, but to me it had that feel about it. Should have received more points.

2005

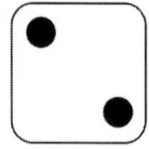

Javine

Palace of Sports, Kyiv, Ukraine was the venue for the 50th Eurovision, on the 19th and 21st May.

Thirty-nine countries participated three more than the previous year, beating the previous record again. Bulgaria and Moldova were first time additions with Hungary returning after a six-year absence.

It was the same format as 2004, with Greece becoming outright winners this year with a song titled *My Number One* performed by Helena Paparizou, this was Greece's first victory in the competition after 31 years of trying.

A couple of incidents worth mentioning, there had been calls for the German entry to quit after it was found that their producer had tried to manipulate the pop charts with mass sales of their artists single, but the calls were rejected.

The other incident was the Ukrainian entry had to be replaced as the song was deemed to contain a political message and EBU stated no politics were/are allowed in songs.

The final took three and a half hours to complete due to the long voting procedure. This caused major disruption amongst television viewing schedules. This led to the voting system which is used today whereby only the top three votes are read out on air and the other scores added automatically.

The UK entry was chosen the same as the previous year through the *Making Your Mind Up 2005* show whereby Sony Music and music experts selected the five acts for the final and the public voted for their favourite.

The winner was Javine, with a song titled *Touch My Fire* written by the artist Javine Dionne Hylton, John Themis and Jonathan Shalit.

Javine an R&B singer already had already tasted success in the UK singles chart and it seemed like the voters had made a a good choice for Eurovision.

In the final Javine performed at number two, with four backing singers/dancers. The up- tempo dance song had a feel of the Middle East about it but didn't seem to go down to well with the public. It was unfortunately another failure for the UK. She finished in twenty-second place with only eighteen points. It did come out later she was suffering with a throat infection before the final, whether that made any difference who knows?

The song did do better in the UK singles chart peaking at eighteen.

Author's Comment:
Boring, lacking anything memorable, her voice did sound a little croaky, so I do believe she had a throat infection. Otherwise another disappointment from the UK.

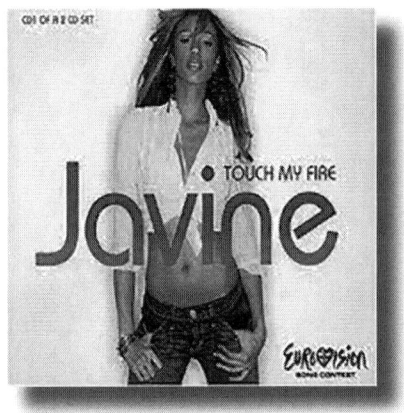

2006

Daz Sampson

The 51st edition of Eurovision took place in Athens, Greece at the Nikos Galis Olympic Indoor Hall on the 18th and 20th May.

Thirty-seven countries took part, Armenia the only newcomer, with Austria, Hungary and Serbia and Montenegro dropping out this year.

The winner was unusually a heavy metal song, *Hard Rock Hallelujah*, performed by Lordi. This was Finland's first win in forty-five years of participation, the longest a country has taken part without success, it was also the first ever hard rock song to win the contest, and first group since Katrina and Waves in 1997.

It is just as well that the UK is one of the *Big Four* and has a direct route to the final, because on the showing of the previous few years results they wouldn't have made it through the semi-final, and that is the same with this year's offering.

Daz Sampson was the winner who would represent the UK, coming through the usual channel, *Making Your Mind Up 2006* TV show final up against six other acts on 4th March.

The winning song *Teenage Life* was also written by the performer Daz Sampson and John Matthews.

The song was a school themed Rap song and he had five young women as backing vocalists, singing and dancing depicted as school girls.

Sampson who incidentally is also a football manager/scout had hit chart success before Eurovision with several rap/dance music groups, but Eurovision just wasn't ready for Sampson and his Rap number and it finished a lowly 19th out of the twenty-four finalists with just twenty-five points.

Sampson was quoted in a documentary in 2013 that Rap maybe was not the best of ideas and believed that Europe was not ready for

Daz Sampson.

Sampson also claims that his performance in Eurovision aledgedly raised the popularity of the contest in the UK leading to extraordinarily high viewing figures in 2006.

The song also did very well in the UK singles charts reaching a respectable high of number eight.

Author's Comment:
I love this, my favourite from the last few years entries.
I believe Sampson was right, Eurovision just wasn't ready for him.

The Daily Telegraph, May 20th, 2006

2007

Scooch

The 52nd Eurovision took place in Helsinki, Finland at the Hartwall Arena, over the 10th and 12th May.

A record breaking forty-two countries took part. The EBU had a limit of forty countries but decided to ignore it. Making it twenty-eight countries taking part in the semi-final and twenty-four in the final.

The Czech Republic and Georgia joined the circus for the first time with Montenegro and Serbia taking part as independent nations for the first time. Austria and Hungary made a return, Monaco dropped out, and hasn't participated ever since.

The winning country was Serbia with the song *Molitva* performed by Marija Marija Šerifovi. This was Serbia's first victory and first as an independent nation, also the first in a native language since Israel with Dana International and the song *Diva*.

The UK's entry after winning through from the six acts taking part in the usual *Making Your Mind Up 2007* TV final was *Flying the Flag (For You)* written by Russ Spencer, Morton Schjolin, Andrew Hill and Paul Tarry and performed by Scooch.

Interesting fact or not? The band's name Scooch comes from a term used to ask someone to move up or along a bench or sofa.

Scooch the British pop group consisted of members Natalie Powers, Caroline Barnes, David Ducasse and Russ Spencer and were formed in 1998.

They were no strangers to competition as they had previously won a contest on the BBC's *Live and Kicking* Saturday morning show in 1999.

They were joined by two backing singers in the final of Eurovision and were dressed as airline cabin crew, using airplane props i.e. refreshment trolleys and airline seats etc.

It didn't seem to make them fly up the leader board though,

The 2000s

performing at number nineteen they accrued a total of nineteen points finishing in twenty-second place.

The song did however reach number five in the UK singles charts, this being their highest charting song, it was also the UK's highest charting Eurovision song since Katrina and Waves *Shine a Light* from 1997.

Author's Comment:
This is what Eurovision is all about, it's criminal that this didn't do better. Okay, the singing is a bit flat, but what a tune... and the costumes... and stage props, a winner every time for me.

Scooch flag at Eurovision

By David Randall

Scooch, Britain's entry for the Eurovision Song contest, proved to be naff, but not nearly naff enough last night as they finished second from last, 249 points behind winners Serbia.

The group's tongue-in-cheek routine, dressed as an airline crew rendering a song called "Flying The Flag (For You)", collected votes from just two of the 42 voting nations, seven from Ireland and 12 from Malta. By contrast, Serbia had the unfair advantage of a decent song (a ballad entitled "Molitva", or "Prayer"), a good singer, Marija Serifovic (who resembled Ugly Betty), and plenty of neighbouring nations to shower them with fraternal votes.

As in previous years, there was the usual round of tactical, not to say strategic, voting.

The Independent, May 13th 2007

The UK in Eurovision - *The Highs and Lows*

 Have your say Should Britain pull out of the Eurovision Song Contest? telegraph.co.uk/news

'Warsaw Pact' leaves Wogan questioning Eurovision future

By Tom Peterkin

TERRY Wogan has threatened to resign as commentator for the Eurovision Song Contest over an Eastern European bloc voting row.

Wogan, whose sardonic commentaries have enlivened the competition for 35 years, said the event was "no longer a musical contest" and suggested that Western European countries should also consider pulling out.

His remarks came at the end of a contest that saw the Russian entrant, Dima Bilan, win the contest in the Serbian capital Belgrade thanks to the support of his Eastern European neighbours.

Wogan's irritation has been fuelled by long-standing suggestions that the voting system is a fix with judges from different countries forming political alliances that overlook any possible musical merit.

The row has escalated recently, with claims that Eastern European countries have formed the musical equivalent of the Warsaw Pact to squeeze out their Western rivals.

The Irish broadcaster, who was given an honorary knighthood in 2005, said that he did not want to take anything away from the Russians, who won the 53rd competition with Bilan's song *Believe* in front of a television audience of 100 million.

However, Wogan said that his producer, Kevin Bishop, was retiring after this year's contest, adding: "He and I have to decide whether we want to do this again."

Yesterday, the Radio 2 presenter said: "Western European participants have to decide whether they want to take part from here on in, because their prospects are poor. I don't want to be presiding over yet another debacle.

Russia were going to be the political winners from the beginning. I think it's tremendously disappointing from the point of view of the United

The Russian winner Dima Bilan (left) finished well ahead of Britain's Andy Abraham (right)

▶ **Is this a competition with nul point?**

Bobby G of **Bucks Fizz**, who won in 1981 with *Making Your Mind Up* said: "Terry must be wanting some publicity. I don't think he'll ever quit.
"Over the last few years everyone has accused the contest of being so political, but if you look at the results it is usually the best three songs that are in the top three."

Ronnie Carroll, who came fourth in 1962 and 1963 with *Say Wonderful Things* and *Ring-a-Ding Girl*, said: "It is absolutely potty. It looks like there's some sort of mad dictatorship going on where the Iron Curtain countries work together."

Bucks Fizz were winners in 1981

Lee Sheridan of **Brotherhood of Man**, who won in 1976 with *Save All Your Kisses for Me*, said: "Some people have suggested an East contest and a West contest but this would go against the object of Eurovision which is to bring countries together."

Bruce Forsyth said: "I agree with Terry. It's not a song contest any more, it's political. It's all so biased, it's developed into a farce. I've stopped watching it in the last couple of years."

Simon Cowell, the pop Svengali, said: "If people enjoy it, that's great, but it's all a bit empty and meaningless."

Max Clifford, the public relations guru, said: "Terry Wogan is spot on. It's all about politics and block voting and nothing to do with the merits of a song. It's like having a World Cup where the results have nothing to do with who scores the most goals."

Kingdom. I'd like to think that the British music industry and [Eurovision organisers] the European Broadcasting Union will find some way of making the voting a little bit fairer." He added: "At least the voting used to be on the songs. Now it is really about national prejudice. As far as the Eastern bloc countries are concerned they are voting for each other."

The British entrant, Andy Abraham, finished joint last on just 14 points with his song *Even* – a far cry from the halcyon days of the Sixties, Seventies and Eighties when acts such as Lulu, Sandie Shaw, Bucks Fizz and Brotherhood of Man dominated the competition.

Wogan had said that the offering by Abraham, a former dustman, was Britain's "best entry for a while".

For the credibility of the show to become a resigning issue for Wogan perhaps seems strange given that his popularity as a host has been based on his cynical witticisms ridiculing the show's descent into farce.

"Who knows what hellish future lies ahead?" he said in his introduction to last year's show in Finland, adding: "Actually, I do. I've seen the rehearsals."

Yesterday, Wogan's stance was supported by showbusiness personalities and Richard Ross, the Liberal Democrat MP, who has tabled a Commons motion calling for BBC funding for the contest to be removed. Britain, France, Germany and Spain are the most generous backers.

Were Wogan to leave, it would be a massive blow to the competition.

For many, his acerbic wit is the only thing that makes it worth watching.

This year's show featured singing pirates, women in false beards and gothic rockers in angel wings. The Bosnian entry was described by Wogan as "the four brides of Frankenstein and a loony with a clothes line".

Yesterday William Hill cut the price of this year being the last appearance of the broadcaster at the Eurovision finals from 4-1 to 3-1. Jonathan Ross is an even money favourite to be the next host.

"Eurovision viewing figures will take a hammering when Terry Wogan leaves because no one is watching it for the music," said Rupert Adams, a spokesman for William Hill.

The Daily Telegraph, May 26th, 2008

Interesting article in The Daily Telegraph Newspaper following the UK's last place, critics of the Eastern Bloc countries coming more and more prominent due to their strategic voting. But hey this is Eurovision, it´s nothing new, we have had this for years with the Scandinavian countries and Greece and Cyprus.

2008

Andy Abraham

Belgrade, Serbia and the Belgrade Arena held the 53rd contest on the 20th, 22nd and 24th May. For the first time there were two semi-finals. Forty-three countries participated breaking 2007's record by one, with Azerbaijan and San Martino coming in and Austria going the other way, Austria did not participate because allegedly they didn't like the semi-final organisation and what they called the politicisation of the contest.

Russia ran out winners with the song *Believe* sung by Dima Bilan.

The show that picks the UK entry once again changed it's name, this time to *Eurovision: Your Decision*, as usual organised by the BBC. Six acts competed in the final and the winner was selected through three rounds by a professional jury and a public televote.

This years winner was Andy Abraham with the song *Even If* written by Andy Abraham, Paul Wilson and Andy Watkins.

Interestingly Abraham was a former refuse collector and bus driver before he became runner up on the TV talent show the *X Factor in 2005*, and his debut album released in 2006 reached number two in the UK album charts.

In the Eurovision final he performed at number twenty-one and was joined on stage by a backing singer, two guitarists, a keyboard player and a drummer. Unfortunately the soul-type song didn't hit the highs with the European juries and Abraham finished last in twenty-fifth place with fourteen points. Only the second time the UK has finished bottom, the last time being 2003. The only consolation was at least it wasn't nul points.

The song didn't do that well in the UK singles chart either, peaking at number sixty-seven.

Author's Comment:
This made me very disappointed, no way did this deserve last place, good tune and good performance from an accomplished singer.

2009

Jade Ewen

Moscow, Russia and the Olimpiysky Arena was the venue for the 54th contest between 12th and 16th May.

Forty-two countries took part, one less than the previous year, Georgia and San Marino didn't take part with Slovakia returning for the first time since 1998.

Russian Gay activists used the contest to promote gay rights in Russia. The leading activist in Russia Nicolai Alekseev announced the Moscow 2009 edition of gay pride would coincide with the final, this didn't go down too well with the Russian authorities and the parade was denied authorisation and any activists would be dealt with toughly.

It was a landslide win for Norway with *Fairytale* performed by Alexander Rybak, with a points tally of 387 out of a possible 492, the highest score in the history of the contest at that time.

A re-introduction of a national jury alongside televoting for the final was reintroduced after there had been criticism in 2007. Televoting had been introduced in 1997 replacing the traditional juries.

The UK entry this year was *It's My Time* written by Andrew Lloyd Webber and Diane Warren and performed by singer (former member of the girl group Sugarbabes) and actress Jade Ewen.

Yet again there was another re-ramp of the selection Show, this time called *Eurovision: Your Country Needs You*. Six acts competed against each other in the national final which consisted of two heats, a semi-final and final, whereby the winning song was selected solely by a public televote.

In the final she was accompanied by four violinists and was later joined by co-composer Andrew Lloyd Webber on the piano.

The song was a relative success considering the previous few years, she came in fifth place with a points tally of 173.

The song peaked at number twenty-seven in the UK singles charts. One thing of note worth mentioning for avid UK Eurofans is that this was the year that Graham Norton became the voice of Eurovision for the UK taking over from the retiring Terry Wogan.

Author's Comment:
Quality singer and song, not sure in 2009 that this genre of entry now fits, but it was entered and she did ok.

Mission to Moscow

After years of British fiascos, Jade Ewen insists that she and Andrew Lloyd Webber can triumph at Eurovision. **James Rampton** meets her

The British are hardly renowned for taking the Eurovision Song Contest seriously. But - hold the arts pages - this year all that is supposedly changing. Andrew Lloyd Webber has been drafted in to beef up the musical credibility of our entry. The result is that at this year's contest in Moscow on Saturday we're not aiming to laugh about coming last, but - shock, horror - trying to win the darn thing.

To that end, Lloyd Webber conducted a four-week audition for singers during January on BBC One's *Your Country Needs You!* The winner was Jade Ewen.

"In the past, Eurovision has had a naff image in the UK because other countries have sent their singing superstars and we haven't," concedes Ewen, a waif-like 21 year-old from Plaistow in the East End of London. "But Andrew and I are trying to turn things around. We've been to 20 European countries promoting our song, which has never been done before. We want people to know that for us this isn't a joke."

Ewen will be singing *It's My Time*, a song composed for the occasion by Lloyd Webber and Diane Warren. "Andrew can change people's view of Eurovision," says Ewen. "He's a globally famous composer. His involvement gives the Eurovision credibility. This is his reputation on the line."

Ewen - who spent much of her youth caring for her blind father and partially blind mother - has been performing for as long as she can recall. "I've always wanted to sing," she says. "My mum says that even as a baby I was dancing along to the commercials in front of the TV. And I remember at the age of four singing *Thumbelina* in a competition. As I looked at my thumb, it was shaking violently with nerves."

But the embryonic star was not to be put off. At the age of 12, Ewen, the eldest of three children, won a scholarship to attend the Sylvia Young Theatre School where her contemporaries included *Hustle*'s Matt Di Angelo and Tom Fletcher from the boy band McFly. After graduating, however, Ewen's career failed to catch fire. She joined a girl band called Trinity Stone who aspired to be a British version of Destiny's Child. But after two and a half years, Trinity Stone turned to dust. She also had cameos in two dramas you'd probably be sacked

Best of British: Jade Ewen, the UK's entrant at this year's Eurovision Song Contest

from Equity for not appearing in: *Casualty* and *The Bill*.

Ewen says she hit a low point this time last year. "I was really depressed," she says. "For 10 months, I'd been trying to get a record contract. I was auditioning loads, but it felt like I kept hitting concrete walls. It got to the point where I was thinking of giving up." But Ewen's luck altered last year when she auditioned for *Myths*, BBC Two's modern-day interpretations of Greek myths for teenagers. The casting director was so impressed that he sent her audition tape off to the producers of *Your Country Needs You!*

The singer admits that she was initially dubious about the project: "I had reservations because a lot of people say it's the end of your career if you do really badly at Eurovision. I was also nervous about doing a reality TV show. If you're uncertain of yourself, there is a risk involved in putting yourself in someone else's hands." In the end, she says, "I reckoned that you can't buy that kind of exposure. I'd never be able to reach that many people otherwise. It's a good platform."

All the same, Ewen was almost paralysed with nerves on the night of the live final of *Your Country Needs You!*, hosted by Graham Norton (who has also taken over from Sir Terry Wogan as our Eurovision commentator).

"I felt sick beforehand," she says. "When I was standing on stage waiting to hear the vote, it felt like 20 minutes before Graham said my name. As soon as I heard it, I cried. I'd never seen my mum crying before, but she was in tears, too. I then had to perform the song again. It's very difficult to sing when you're blubbering and your nose is running. Still, it was good TV!"

The question is what Ewen will do after Eurovision; most singers who represent Britain soon vanish from the public eye. But Ewen has a contract to record an album with Universal, and says she wants to learn the piano: "Maybe I'll ask Andrew to teach me…"

She's clearly delighted by the prospect of representing the UK on Saturday. There's only one thing that worries her. "Fame scares me a little," she says. "I do this because I love singing, not because I want to be a celebrity. All of a sudden, everyone knows who I am and has an opinion about me. I'm not used to that."

But, she adds hastily, "I will never take myself too seriously. I won't turn into a diva. My mum would soon slap me down if I did. Everyone in Plaistow knows me and they would be very quick to say, 'Who do you think you are?'"

+ *Eurovision Song Contest 2009* is on BBC One on Saturday at 8.00pm

*Well what can you say?
To say the 2000s has been a failure is an understatement.
Wasted opportunities to promote the best of what the UK has to offer in the music industry just hasn't happened.
We had become a bit of an embarrassment on the continent!*

The 2010s and onwards

2010-2023

2010

Josh Dubovie

The 55th Eurovision took place in Oslo, Norway at the Telenor Arena over the 25, 27 and 29 May.

Thirty-nine countries took part with Georgia returning with Andorra, Czech Republic, Hungary and Montenegro dropping out.

Germany won this time with the song *Satellite* performed by Lena. This was Germany's second win but their first as a unified country.

This year the voting in the semi-finals was brought into line nearer the final with televoting and Juries splitting fifty percent each of the votes.

The UK entry was picked the same way as the previous year through the *Eurovision: Your Country Needs You 2010* show by the BBC.

The winner Josh Dubovie with a song titled *That Sounds Good to Me* and written by Pete Waterman, Mick Stock and Steve Crosby, Dubovie thought the song was that good he could go on to win the whole competition with it.

Well that didn't quite happen, in fact he ended up the opposite end of the leaderboard in last place twenty-fifth with an enormous points total of ten.

This was the third time the UK finished in last place.

Before the final the national press had described the song as naff, one paper describing the song as the pop equivalent of re-processed meat. The bookmakers were not that impressed either giving the song odds of 125-1, that being the longest odds ever given to a UK entry.

It faired just as bad in the UK singles charts barely registering at 179.

Author's Comment:
Got to agree with the critics with this one, not a good start to the new decade.

2011

Blue

Eurovision made its way to Düsseldorf, Germany where at Düsseldorf Arena over the 10th, 12th and 14th May forty-three countries took part, equalling the record set in 2008. San Marino made a comeback, Italy also made a long-awaited comeback, last time they took part was way back in 1997. Due to this Italy joined the *Big Four* and they became known as the *Big Five*. Also Hungary and Austria returned, with Slovakia dropping out due to financial reasons.

Azerbaijan won with a song called *Running Scared* performed by Ell and Nikki, the country's first win after only taking part for four years. Strange enough it was also the first time a male-female duo won the contest since way back in 1963.

With a break from the selection process of the previous few years the BBC decided that they internally select an act. This was mainly due to the poor results and decreasing public interest after record low viewing figures for the 2010 contest. The Beeb thought they could get success by selecting the boyband Blue with a song titled *I Can* written by Duncan James, Lee Ryan, Ciaron Bell, Ben Collier, Ian Hope and StarSign.

Blue with band members Simon Webbe, Duncan James, Anthony Costa and Lee Ryan were used to success, having had major hits in the early 2000s, before taking a prolonged break from 2004 and reforming in 2011 to represent the UK.

The BBC was slammed by the media for it's arrogance by out of touch bureaucrats by imposing a band and a song on the British public. The band were described in some of the media as an outdated 90s boyband and the song shocking.

Even with all the criticism the band were still fourth favourites with the bookmakers.

Blue made international appearances promoting the song and a documentary was made about the lead up to Eurovision. All this

The UK in Eurovision - *The Highs and Lows*

being good publicity for the song.

Blue performed in fourteenth position in the final and finished in eleventh place with 100 points.

The final was watched by an average of 9.54 million viewers in the UK more than double the viewers from the previous year and making it the most watched Eurovision since 1999.

I Can peaked at number sixteen in the UK singles charts and made the top ten in Germany, Austria and Switzerland and charted in several other European countries.

Author's Comment:
Even a well-known boyband couldn't persuade the European public to give the UK a winner, but to be fair to the public the song was garbage.

Kitsch crown: Azerbaijan's Ell/Nikki celebrate their Eurovision victory

Eurovision is still such a joy

HOORAY for Azerbaijan, both of Jedward, Graham Norton and the joke that never seems to die. Everything that could possibly be said about the Eurovision Song Contest has long since been said; its political significance has been analysed to death, and it's bathed beneath so many layers of meta-irony that we've all long since lost any sense of what level we're supposed to be enjoying it on. But this Eurovision did spawn a new joke, and one I wish I could claim credit for. Q: What's blue and can't sing? A: Blue.

The Evening Standard, May 16th, 2011

The 2010s

2012

Engelbert Humperdinck

Baku Crystal Hall, Baku, Azerbaijan hosted the 57th Eurovision over the 22nd, 24th and 26th May.

Forty-two countries took part. Montenegro returned, Armenia withdrew for security reasons due to an ongoing conflict with the host country, and Poland dropped out due to financial restraints.

Leading up to the contest there were protests by many groups due to the host nations human rights record.

There were also tensions with Iran who objected to Azerbaijan hosting the competition, condemning them for anti-Islamic behaviour labelling the contest a gay parade. This led to protest by Azerbaijanians outside the Iranian embassy in Baku demanding an apology.

Sweden were the victors with one of Eurovision's now iconic songs *Euphoria* performed by Loreen.

Again the BBC took it upon itself and internally selected the artist and song to represent the UK in Baku. They chose the well-known and mega successful international artist Engelbert Humperdinck with a song titled *Love Will Set You Free* written by Martin Terefe and Sacha Skarbek.

He has been described as one of the finest balladeers around with worldwide hits from way back in the mid-60s up to and past the 2001's.

This seemed like a really good call from the BBC and Humperdinck himself had quoted he was very proud of the song and having the nation behind him and was looking forward to the rollercoaster ride that is Eurovision.

Fourth favourite with the bookmakers, he was drawn to perform first in the final and performed with a guitarist, James Bryan, alongside male and female ballet dancers.

Unfortunately once again it wasn't received very well by the mass voting public and juries and finished in twenty-fifth place out of twenty-six with twelve points.

The single released peaked at number sixty in the UK charts.

Also the viewing figures were down on the previous year with approximately seven million, a couple of million down, although there was a major sporting event going on at the same time.

After the contest the political question rose its ugly head again in the media, and there were calls from several media personalities for the BBC to withdraw from the contest, as they now felt it was too politically influenced.

Author's Comment:
I know in some circles people think that there is a political bias towards the UK, I personally believe that if the song is good enough they will vote for it, this song just wasn't, simple as that. Just because the BBC choose a superstar to represent the UK doesn't mean the song will automatically race up the scoreboard.

Eurovision and Engelbert Humperdinck: one guilty pleasure deserves another

'I will proudly represent my country in song'

WILLIAM LANGLEY
LONDON DAILY TELEGRAPH

Europe is coming apart. The stitches are popping from Tromso to Thebes, and unity means no more than everyone going broke together. Still, there's always the Eurovision Song Contest. As a metaphor of indivisibility, the annual schmaltzfest has done decent service, but today is looking more like the white flag of a continent preparing to face the music. Or, as Britain's latest contestant might put it, The Last Waltz.

In a pleasing sense, Engelbert Humperdinck and the Eurovision Song Contest are ideally suited. The contest draws a TV audience of 100 million people, although no one ever admits to watching it, while Humperdinck has sold 150 million albums, but it is impossible to find anybody who owns one.

"I am so thrilled to have been asked to represent the U.K. at Eurovision 2012," the 75-year-old, Leicestershire-raised ex-factory hand declared on his website last week. "I will proudly represent my country in song." Maximum points for patriotic spirit, then, but how – in what might be called this mature phase of his career – is Humperdinck going to compete with hot-stepping troupes of strobe-lit Moldavians and Latvians, and get around the

Engelbert Humperdinck is only the second septuagenarian to compete in the Eurovision Song Contest.

Scandinavian block-voting?

It's a tough gig, but Humperdinck has known worse. All his life, he has lived in the shadows of others. For several years he was marooned on the pub circuit, living in an apartment with no furniture and watching others get the breaks. When his finally came, he found himself in the same stable as Tom Jones, who, on the preferred measurement of post-show panty accumulations, was judged to be marginally more successful. When Humperdinck moved from Britain to America, he distinguished himself by growing mutton-chop sideburns, only to have the idea stolen by Elvis, who is still credited with thinking of it. "I never begrudged him that," Humperdinck graciously tells interviewers. "He was always my favourite performer."

What his rivals struggle to match is his workload. Two hundred concerts a year is taking it easy for The Hump. This week will find him in Dubai, followed by two nights in Beirut, then back to the U.S., on to South America, and later in the year he'll be back in Britain. Pretty much every show is sold out.

Eurovision may be a challenge of a different order; if only because the event's galactic weirdness makes it unusually hard to predict – or prepare for – a win. Drowned up at a 1955 broadcasting shindig in Monte Carlo, the contest was originally seen both as a way of brightening up the mood of postwar Europe and a technical experiment in live multinational television. The idea took a while to catch on, but by the '60s was pulling in big audiences and had established a musical genre vaguely known as Europop, a world-beyond-irony mix of high-camp melodic goo that bore only a distant resemblance to the national music of the participating countries.

Why Humperdinck? By any measure, his candidacy is a gamble. The oldest winner to date was Denmark's Jorgen Olsen, who was just the wrong side of 50 when he landed the prize in 2000 with his brother Niels. No other septuagenarian (apart from an oddball Croatian rapper who finished nowhere in 2008) has ever taken part. The word from the BBC is that its selectors are fed up with sending bottom-of-the-barrel reality-show rejects, and are prepared to try something radically different.

At least Humperdinck has experience. Lots of it. He was 9 years old, and still known as Arnold Dorsey, when he learned to play the saxophone, and by his mid-teens was playing in pubs around the family home. One night, when he was 17, he was at the Bond Street Working Men's Club in Leicester. Someone bought him a beer, "and it gave me the confidence to get up and sing," he recalls. "Afterwards, these agents came over and said, 'Who's your agent?'"

He soldiered on – as Gerry Dorsey, which he thought sounded more sophisticated – but it wasn't until 1966, when he attracted the interest of Gordon Mills, the powerful pop manager who had steered Jones to stardom, that his prospects began looking up. Figuring there were already too many retro-smoothie lounge acts competing for business, Mills decided that his new signing needed a gimmick. The one he came up with was turning Dorsey into Engelbert Humperdinck – the name of a little-remembered German composer.

The effect was immediate. Humperdinck was invited to appear on the television variety show Sunday Night at the London Palladium, where he delivered a rendition of the 1946 smoocher Release Me. It rocketed straight to No. 1, fending off the Beatles' double-sider Penny Lane/Strawberry Fields Forever, and went on to become one of the biggest-selling singles in history.

The Hump has been a big name – in every sense – ever since. Can he hold his own against the vowel-mangled warblings of upstart Estonians and knee-pumping Azerbaijani boogie-boys? The signs look promising. Within minutes of the announcement that Humperdinck would take part in Eurovision, bookmaker William Hill cut the odds of a British win from 25/1 to 16/1, making the U.K. fourth favourites.

2013

Bonnie Tyler

Once again we are back in Sweden, Malmo at the Malmo Arena on the 14th, 16th and 18th May.

Thirty-nine countries participated with Armenia returning, Bosnia and Herzegovina, Portugal, Turkey and Slovakia withdrawing. Strangely Turkey and Slovakia have yet to return.

Outright winners were Denmark with *Only Teardrops* performed by Emmelie de Forest. Denmark seems to like Sweden as this was the second time they had won here.

The BBC once again chose the UK entry with a song *Believe in Me* written by Desmond Child, Lauren Christy and Christopher Braide. The chosen artist to perform the song was superstar Welsh singer Bonnie Tyler with a string of home and international hits behind her.

Once again the BBC thinks by picking a well-known superstar to represent the UK it will do well. I'm afraid the audience is not that naive, it is a much younger audience these days, and these tactics just don't cut the mustard.

Back to the song and the lyrics depict the singer telling her lover who doesn't believe in religion or love, to just believe in her.

I don't think the media had much belief in the song either, as it received mixed reviews, the music press even calling it mediocre for someone of Tyler's stature.

She performed at fifteen in the final and amassed twenty-three points and finished in nineteenth place. The music press justifying their belief that the song wasn't good enough for Tyler.

Tyler speaking after the votes came in, said that despite her final score the experience had been "fantastic".

She said: "I got the feeling tonight that I got at the Grammy awards, I'm sure a lot of people will be disappointed on my behalf but I have really enjoyed my Eurovision experience."

"I did the best that I could do with a great song. I don't feel down and I'm ready to party."

"The songs at the top of the table totally deserve to be up there. Of course I would have liked to bring it back to the UK but it's been a night to remember."

The single didn't do much better either peaking at number 93 and didn't chart anywhere else.

Author's Comment:
Terrible song for a proven music superstar. One to forget.

Eurovision
AT LEAST GRAHAM'S A WINNER

By **ROBERT MEAKIN**

Ever since Sir Terry Wogan handed over the baton in 2009, there has never been any doubt that Graham Norton and the Eurovision Song Contest are a perfect match. Making his fifth appearance as BBC 1's resident commentator – this year in the Swedish city of Malmo – Norton once again played the role of mischievous gatecrasher, taking delicious aim at the array of hopefuls, presenters and merry idiots on Saturday night.

While 2012 was all about "Poor Engelbert Humperdinck" this year's ever-present Nortonism soon became "Poor Bonnie Tyler" as it quickly became apparent that the decision to entrust British hopes with a well-known singer from yesteryear had once again failed to cut the mustard. The veteran Welsh star, who performed the optimistic ditty "Believe In Me", finished the evening 19th out of 26 – in fairness an improvement on Humperdinck, who memorably had to endure the humiliation of coming second from bottom.

As the vanquished Bonnie no doubt prepared to knock back another Cinzano and lemonade as the votes piled up in favour of Denmark, Azerbaijan and Ukraine, our host helpfully observed: "I'm no Carol Vorderman, but I don't think the UK can win now." During the lengthy voting process, Norton would occasionally feel duty-bound to instil a sense of kitsch drama. "Azerbaijan could still do this," he assured us, before Denmark's Emmelie de Forest sealed victory.

Eurovision without Graham Norton? Surely that's when we all finally switch off.

The Independent,
May 20th, 2013

2014

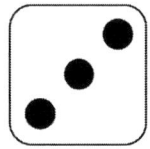

Molly

The 59th Eurovision stayed in Scandinavia with a short hop over to Copenhagen, Denmark and the B&W Hallerne, a former shipyard with the surrounding area transformed into Eurovision Island, and it took place on the dates 6th, 8th and 10th May.

Thirty-seven countries participated in the contest — the smallest number since 2006. Poland and Portugal returned with Bulgaria, Croatia, Cyprus and Serbia dropping out.

The winner being Austria, with the song *Rise Like a Phoenix* performed by Conchita Wurst. The last time Austria won was in 1966. This happens to be the longest break between victories for any country at this time, mind you the way the UK results are going we could break that record.

A point worth mentioning, there was a record for viewing figures, a total of over 195 million was reported tuning in to this year's contest.

Once again the BBC hand-picked the artist to represent the UK. This time singer and songwriter Molly Smitten-Downes was chosen. Going by just her first name Molly, she had already had chart success with the Dance music project Stunt with a collaboration with Sash!.

The song that Molly was going to perform was *Children of the Universe* and was written by Molly and Anders Hansson who she had collaborated with previously on a couple of projects.

The entry seemed to excite the media and was fairly well received from the music critics. The critic for the newspaper *The Daily Mirror* said: "Molly's voice has such a powerful tone to it – combined with the thumping beat, it makes you want to sing along – even if you don't know the lyrics. Overall it's the best thing we've produced since Gina G's 'Ooh Ahh... Just a Little Bit' (8th place 1996) which is a very good thing."

Molly was drawn to perform last in the final, twenty-sixth position. She was supported by a drummer Joe Yoshida, and four backing singers Lincoln Jean-Marie, Katie Holmes (not the American actress), Victoria Beaumont and Sharleen Linton.

The song was one of the bookmakers' favourites to win the competition, but as usual that doesn't always follow suit, and this was no exception, she finished in seventeenth place with a tally of only forty points.

The song did however peak at number twenty-three in the UK charts and was a minor hit in some European countries.

Author's Comment:
I personally don't hold the song in such high regard as the media did, probably finished where it deserved.

2015

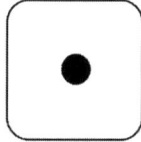

Electric Velvet

Over to Austria for the 60th contest, taking place in Vienna at the Wiener Stadthalle during the dates of 19th, 21st and 23rd May.

Forty countries participated with Cyprus, Czech Republic and Serbia returning and due to an ongoing political crises in Ukraine connected to the Russo-Ukrainian War they opted out.

Due to it being the 60th contest, Australia was allowed to make a guest appearance, but they were put straight through to the final so as to not upset the chances of the other European countries fighting it out for a place.

Eurovision is extremely popular in Australia with very high proportional viewing figures for the show. It was supposed to be a one-off appearance, but as we know, they are now allowed to participate as normal with everybody else from 2016 onwards, that is competing through the semi-finals.

Now the winner was Sweden with the song *Heroes* performed by Måns Zelmerlöw, the second win for Sweden in three years.

Once again Eurovision was proving to be a success with viewing figures beating the previous year from 195 million to 197 million.

The internal selection process by the BBC this year chose the song *Still in Love with You* written by David Mindel and Adrian Bax White and performed by duo Electro Velvet which is made up of Alex Larke and Bianca Nicholas. The song is 1920's swing music influenced with a modern spin to it.

Nicholas was no stranger to contests as she had appeared in both TV knock-out shows *The X-Factor* and *The Voice UK*. She had also performed with Will Young and performed in front of members of the Royal Family. A single she released in 2011 had also made it into the top 100. She doesn't mind people knowing that she also suffers from Cystic Fibrosis.

In 2014 Larke was working as a teacher in a special needs school. (He now fronts a tribute Rolling Stones band and tours the world).

The song wasn't well received and criticised in the media as being nightmarish, unforgettable and a bit of a balls up.

The song was chosen to perform at number five in the final, keeping with the song's 1920's feel they performed in costumes keeping with that era and were joined by four backing singers Scarlette Douglas, Sophie Carmen Jones, Chris Arias and Ryan Helseltine.

It wasn't expected to win and didn't disappoint, finishing in a lowly twenty-fourth place with a grand total of only five points.

The single release didn't do much better either, just breaking into the top 120, peaking at 114.

Author's Comment:
Not much you can say really, just grit your teeth and smile!!

2016

Joe and Jake

Back in Stockholm, Sweden for the 61st Eurovision at the Globe Arena during the dates of 10th, 12th and 14th May.

Forty-two countries took part with Bosnia and Herzegovina, Bulgaria, Croatia and Ukraine returning with Australia allowed to take part after the guest appearance the previous year. Portugal didn't enter and Romania were disqualified due to non payment of debts owed by their broadcaster to the EBU.

Ukraine were the outright winners with a song titled *1944* and performed by the artist Jamala. Australia who only debuted the previous year came in second place.

For the first time the contest was broadcast live in the USA, which boosted the viewing figures to a record breaking 204 million viewers worldwide, smashing the record set in 2015 by over five million.

Eurovision was now proving a huge global hit.

There was a change to the voting system again this year. I will simplify the change. The jury from each country would award two sets of points from 1-8, then 10 and 12, one from their professional jury and one from televoting. The televoting from all the countries would be pooled, so after the professional juries had announced their results, the combined televoting would be announced for each country.

After the disappointing results of the last few contests whereby the BBC had internally picked the artists they reverted back to a TV selection show again *Eurovision: You Decide,* six acts competed in the final and the public voted for the winner.

You're Not Alone was the winning song written by Matt Schwartz, Justin J. Benson and S. Kanes performed by Joe and Jake, full names Joe Woolford and Jake Shakeshaft. They formed the duo after meeting on the TV talent show *The Voice UK.*

The catchy pop style song had reasonably good reviews amongst the media and was predicted to do well.

The duo performed at number twenty-five in the final, but once again the media was proved wrong, they finished well down the leader board in twenty-fourth place with sixty-two points.

The release of the single peaked at number eighty-one in the UK singles charts.

Author's Comment:
This deserved much better, a really feel good catchy pop song, very well performed by the duo.

Leave or stay with Euro vision?

WITH Eurovision on our screens tomorrow night – just over a month before the EU referendum – will the song contest swing hearts and minds? We asked the in/out campaigns.

"If the panel of judges had a vote in this referendum, we are confident they would give the Leave campaigns nul points for losing the economic argument so comprehensively," was Stronger In's stern response. "We expect our supporters will take a break from campaigning," they added, "and come together on the night to celebrate Britain's place in Europe." How heartwarming – but what about the Brexiteers? Surely they'll have the TV turned off, while leafing through the Magna Carta?

"We're all lovers of Eurovision here in the Leave.EU press office," we were told. "We doubt it will influence the referendum but if our entry, Joe and Jake [pictured], don't win perhaps our next campaign will be against the unfair bias within Eurovision." But what of Vote Leave? They did not return our emails.

The Evening Standard, May 13th, 2016

2017

Lucie Jones

Forty-two countries took part at the International Exhibition Centre, Kyiv, Ukraine on 9th, 11th and 13th May with Portugal and Romania returning and Bosnia and Herzegovina and Russia dropping out.

Russia's artist Julia Samoylova was banned from entering Ukraine because she had travelled directly from Russia to Crimea, a region annexed by Russia in 2014, to give a performance. This made her Ukraine entry illegal.

The winning entry was Portugal with *Amar pelos dois* performed by Salvador Sobral, this being Portugal's first win in Eurovision and first top five placing in fifty-three years of trying. The longest winless run by any country in Eurovision history.

The BBC continued with the same concept as the previous year with the TV show *Eurovision: You Decide* whereby six acts go head to head and the winner is chosen by the public.

The winning song was a super ballad *Never Give Up on You* by Daniel Salcedo, Emmelie de Forest and Lawrie Martin and performed by Welsh singer, musical theatre actress Lucie Jones, full name Lucie Bethan Jones.

Jones was not unfamiliar with competition as she had taken part in the talent show *The X Factor UK* in 2009 where she finished in eighth place.

In the final she performed at number eighteen, but only scored 111 points and finished in fifteenth place, a very disappointing result considering all the plaudits the critics gave it and even the bookmakers fancied it.

She allegedly said in an interview after the final that Brexit had affected the result but in a later interview with the BBC she backtracked on that comment and said she had noticed no affect from Brexit or the attitude towards her from fellow artists or fans at Eurovision.

The released single reached number seventy-three in the UK

The UK in Eurovision - *The Highs and Lows*

singles charts.

There was a drop in viewing figures this year, 22 million fewer than 2016 with 182 million viewers worldwide.

With her super voice she went onto appear in many musical stage adaptations from *Les Misérables* to *We Will Rock You*.

Author's Comment:
I have no idea how this song never finished in the top 10, if not top five, an injustice if ever there was one. Was Lucie's alleged comment correct? Did Brexit affect the result? Who knows!

Voices

Eurovision's indifference to Brexit is hard to stomach

Given the UK's wretched recent results, 15th was a respectable placing for Lucie Jones (Rex)

MATTHEW NORMAN

"Good evening, London, this is Europe calling. First of all, guys, thanks for putting on such a great show these last 44 years. It's been amazing. And now here are the results of the European jury. And the result is... we couldn't care less about Brexit."

So much for the speculation that the continent would take its chance to humiliate the UK at Eurovision. In the event, it was far worse than that. Rage and resentment we can live with. Irrelevance is an infinitely heavier cross to bear.

The Independent, May 15th, 2017

2018

SuRie

Lisbon Arena, Lisbon, Portugal was the venue for the 63rd edition of Eurovision over the dates 8th, 10th and 12th May. Forty-three countries participated equalling the previous record set in 2008 and 2011. The additional country to equal the record this year was Russia, with no countries dropping out.

Israel won with the song *Toy* performed by Netta.

Once again the UK entry was chosen through *Eurovision: You Decide,* the winning song from the six acts was *Storm* written by Nicole Blair, Gil Lewis and Sean Hargreaves and performed by English singer songwriter SuRie, real name Sussanna Marie Cork. SuRie is a combination of her first names Sussanna Marie.

She has had previous experience of the Eurovision, as in 2015 she was a backing vocalist and dancer for the Belgium entry Loic Nottet with *Rhythm Inside* and also musical director for Blanche's *City Lights* in 2017.

SuRie performed at position nine in the final, and was joined by three backing singers, Charlotte Churchman, Debby Bracknell and Mark De-Lisser.

A major incident occurred during SuRie's performance. She was interrupted by a stage invader who grabbed the microphone from her and shouted "Modern Nazis of the UK media, we demand freedom! War is not peace!" before he was removed by security and taken into police custody. Although shaken SuRie was able to finish her performance. In fact she seemed to be buoyed by the stage invasion. She upped her performance and the audience also responded, singing along with her.

She was offered the opportunity to perform the song again but declined. Her team were proud of her performance and deemed it unnecessary.

In an interview with her the next morning on the ITV show *This Morning* she revealed she had accrued some bruises on her hands

The UK in Eurovision - *The Highs and Lows*

and shoulder where the stage invader had barged into her to grab the microphone, but she stated that she wasn't seriously hurt by the incident.

Unfortunately the stage invasion didn't give her any sympathy votes and she finished a lowly twenty-fourth place with forty-eight points.

The single peaked at number fifty on the UK singles charts.

A reported worldwide audience of around 186 million saw the Eurovision this year, 4 million more than 2017.

Author's Comment:
I agree with her not performing the song again, and I thought the performance improved after the stage invader. Should have done better, wasn't a bad song.

The Independent, May 12th, 2018

The 2010s

12 th May 2018, Portugal, Lisbon: Great Britain's SuRie is escorted off stage after a man (not shown) tried to take the microphone from her at the finals of the 63rd Eurovision Song Contest. Photo: Jörg Carstensen/dpa

The UK in Eurovision - *The Highs and Lows*

2019

Michael Rice

The 64th Eurovision was held in Tel Aviv, Israel at the Expo Tel Aviv over the dates of 14th, 16th and 18th May.

Forty-one countries took part with Bulgaria and Ukraine dropping out.

The contest wasn't without controversy this year with the Israeli-Palestinian conflict ongoing in the background of the event. This led to a demonstration from pop star Madonna in the interval entertainment and during the contest from the Icelandic entrant Hatari.

The winner this year was the Netherlands with a song entitled *Arcade* performed by Duncan Laurence.

The UK entry was chosen through the *Eurovision: You Decide* format. The winner chosen from the six acts by the public and jury was pop singer Michael Rice with the song *Bigger than Us* written by Laurell Baker, Anna-Klara Folin, John Lundvik and Jonas Thander.

Seems to be a bit of a trend, time and time again we see that the artists chosen to represent the UK have come through previous competitions. Rice had won the first series of BBC One's singing competion *All Together Now* in 2018 and had also appeared in the eleventh series of the *X Factor* in 2014.

Rice was drawn to appear at position sixteen in the final and was supported by five backing vocalists Anna Sahlene, Chin Simon, Desta Zion Wilson, Linda Pritchard and Melanie Wehbe. Incidentally Sahlene had previously represented Estonia in Eurovision coming third in 2002.

Unfortunately third place was a long way off, Rice came in last in twenty-sixth position with a grand total of eleven points. Another disaster for the UK.

The single faired a little better peaking at twenty-seven in the UK singles charts.

This year also saw the four million viewing figures gained from 2018 disappear and an estimated 182 million watched this year.

Author's Comment:
I liked this song, and so did a ton of other people if you read the comments on the official Eurovision website and the fans sites. Not sure how this didn't finish higher up the leaderboard, definitely deserved more.

Eurovision hasn't lost its boom bang-a-bang completely: it's still a must-watch TV extravaganza, and Saturday's final in Tel Aviv will be closely fought this year. If you're after a hard-hitting, eye-opening message (and possibly hearing damage) that is guaranteed to shake things up, look no further than Iceland and performance art collective Hatari. "Hate will prevail," they squawk (in Icelandic) dressed in Game of Thrones-meets-BDSM bondage gear. It's an anti-capitalist plethora of pleather. Icelandic kids are loving it, and spiked collars are, apparently, flying out of the shops in Reykjavik.

Australia's popular visual belter is also destined for all eternity to feature in video clip compilations of "crazy" Eurovision moments. Zero Gravity is pop opera tinged with Kate Bush, in which singer Kate Miller-Heidke, left, resembles Glinda the Good Witch on acid as she loopily boings around in mid-air atop a bendy pole (thankfully, not a bendy Pole) backed by two similarly swaying wraith-like women.

And what about the UK? We have Michael Rice, aged 21, from Hartlepool. He won BBC talent show All Together Now and owns a waffle and milkshake business, after a stint working at McDonald's. Promisingly, his song Bigger Than Us is co-penned by John Lundvik, who sings and co-wrote the fancied Swedish entry. If he wins, he will be the first black solo act to do so. Both are uplifting anthems with gospel-y backing. The hot favourite is the Netherlands' minimalist mid-tempo ballad Arcade.

So, you might ask, with all this political signalling, where is the timely climate-change song this year? The UK actually came sixth with the green-themed Give a Little Love Back to the World back in 1990 but perhaps Greta Thunberg can get her mum (Sweden's representative in 2009) to do something next year.

● *The Eurovision Song Contest second semi-final is on BBC Four tonight at 8pm, and the final is on BBC One on Saturday at 8pm*

Mark Cook

The Evening Standard, May 16th, 2019

The UK in Eurovision - *The Highs and Lows*

No contest: In corona era, Eurovision seeks to unite Europe

By MIKE CORDER
ASSOCIATED PRESS

THE HAGUE, Netherland — This was no contest.

Shut down by the coronavirus crisis, Europe's annual musical spectacular that pits countries against one another instead sought to unite them Saturday.

The Eurovision Song Contest whose final was scheduled for Saturday night was canceled amid restrictions aimed at reining in the global pandemic.

So rather than judging songs from 41 artists from Albania to the United Kingdom and having countries allocate points to elect a winner, organizers created a two-hour show called "Eurovision: Europe Shine A Light" that was broadcast in more than 40 countries.

Underscoring the effects of the coronavirus, the show opened with a montage of videos of the deserted streets of European cities before cutting to an almost empty studio in the Netherlands.

It was a stark contrast to the frenetic scenes of flag-waving, screaming fans that form the backdrop for normal Eurovision finales.

Part of the Ahoy convention center in the port city of Rotterdam that was to have hosted the contest was transformed earlier this year into a makeshift care center to ease strain on regular hospitals treating COVID-19 patients.

At the end of the show, it was announced that Ahoy and Rotterdam will host the 2021 Eurovision Song Contest.

Saturday's show featured appearances by past favorites as well as the artists that were to have taken part in this year's competition jointly performing 1997's winning song, "Love Shine a Light," made famous by Katrina and the Waves.

From its humble beginnings in 1956, the contest has become a vector of camp and kitsch with almost 200 million viewers tuning in for the finale.

Johnny Logan of Ireland, who won twice as a singer and once as a writer, opened Saturday's show with a performance of his 1980 winning song, "What's Another Year," accompanied by Eurovision fans on screens like a Zoom meeting and the three Dutch presenters of the show. Organizers called it "a huge Eurovision choir."

Måns Zelmerlöw of Sweden sang his 2015 winning song, "Heroes," this year dedicated to health care workers battling the virus.

Snippets of the 41 songs that were to have taken part in this year's contest were played throughout the show with recorded messages from the performers.

The Mamas, Sweden's entry, urged viewers to stay safe and wash their hands.

One of Sweden's brightest musical stars, Bjorn Ulvaeus of ABBA, paid tribute to the contest that catapulted him and the band to global fame after their song "Waterloo" won in 1974.

"It still remains one of the most genuinely joyous events of the TV year — and it's so disarmingly European," he said in a video message. "It so allows you to escape and be happy — even forget about the coronavirus for a little while."

Leader Telegram, May 18th, 2020

2020

Covid-19

The 65th edition of Eurovision was planned to take place in Rotterdam, Netherlands at the Rotterdam Ahoy during the dates of 12th, 14th and 16th May. Unfortunately the event was cancelled on 18th March due to the COVID-19 pandemic.

This was the first time in the contest's 64 year history that the contest hasn't been held.

In place of the contest it was decided that a replacement show would be broadcast around the world this show being *Eurovision: Europe Shine a Light* to showcase all the selected entries from the countries that should have participated.

Before the competition's cancellation the UK entry had already been chosen. After the last few disappointments the BBC ditched the *Eurovision: You Decide* format and went back to internally picking the UK representative. James Newman a singer songwriter was the chosen artist with a song titled *My Last Breath* written by James Newman, Ed Drewett, Adam Argyle and Iain James.

Newman had previously won a Brit Award for his part in co-writing the British single of the year 2014. He has also been a featured vocalist on several dance song hits.

Unfortunately he wouldn't get to perform his song this year in the Netherlands.

2021

James Newman

After the cancellation last year, which should have been the 65th edition, this year became the 65th edition and the same country and venue from 2020 hosted the event, in the Netherlands, Rotterdam at the Rotterdam Ahoy during the dates of 18th, 20th and 22nd May.

Thirty-nine countries participated, Ukraine returned, Hungary, Montenegro, Armenia and Belarus didn't take part.

The songs which were going to be performed in 2020 were not allowed to be re-entered but you could send the same artist with a different song and 26 countries chose to do this.

Due to the still ongoing pandemic, precautions were taken and it was regulated that an audience of no more than 3,500 people attend the semi-finals and final and all the audience members must have certified proof of testing covid negative.

The winner this year was Italy with *Zitti e buoni* performed by Måneskin.

The UK entry was the same artist as 2020, James Newman but with a different song titled *Embers,* an upbeat dance pop song written by James Newman, Conor Blake, Danny Shah, Tom Hollings and Samuel Brennan.

In an interview Newman was quoted that he felt everybody needed to party after the relief of covid restrictions being relaxed and the song was supposed to reflect on that. It received mixed reviews from the media, one journalist even reporting that the song should be good enough to avoid the dreaded nul points. How wrong was that?

He was drawn to perform at number nine in the final, unfortunately the song didn't go down very well with the voting countries public and it was another disaster for the UK, Newman finished in last place, with for only the second time in UK Eurovision history with nul points. He received the support from the public on the night with boos from the audience when he received nul points. He also was applauded by the other artists in the backstage greenroom taking the whole disappointment very well. A credit to Newman and the UK.

On another note, it was the fifth time the UK had finished last.

The single made it to number forty-seven in the UK singles chart and was a minor hit in Europe and even went platinum in Denmark.

Viewing figures were estimated at 183 million an increase from the previous year.

Author's Comment:
A bit harsh on Newman, the song wasn't that bad, and his performance on the night was good.

The UK in Eurovision - *The Highs and Lows*

2022

Sam Ryder

The 66th edition of Eurovision transferred the baton to Italy, Turin and the PalaOlimpico over the dates of 10th, 12th and 14th May.

Forty countries participated this year with Armenia and Montenegro returning and Russia was excluded due to the invasion of Ukraine.

The winner overwhelmingly was Ukraine with the song *Stefania* performed by Kalush Orchestra. The song was performed solely in Ukrainian and was the first song with hip-hop elements to win the contest.

The winning song wasn't the original choice for the final. The winner of the Ukrainian national selection was artist Alina Pash with the song *Shadows of Forgotten Ancestors*. Due to a violation that she had entered Crimea from Russian territory in 2015. Her team had counterfeited her travel documents so she could take part in the selection process. After it was proven she had in fact been in Russian territory she withdrew from the competition before being excluded. Therefore the runner-up Kalush Orchestra took her place.

The BBC decided to internally pick the artist to represent the UK. Finally they chose an exciting and exceptionally talented British singer-songwriter, Sam Ryder with his song *Space Man* which he wrote along with Max Wolfgang and Amy Wadge.

Ryder's early music career saw him front a couple of rock bands. Firstly US rock band Blessed by a Broken Heart. He then went on to front a Canadian band Close Your Eyes. After leaving the band he returned to the UK whereby he worked with his father in the construction industry. Still pursuing music he recorded an album in Nashville, USA, but it was never released and in 2019 he was in fact working as a wedding singer until the outbreak of Covid and lockdown.

During lockdown he started posting material on *Tik Tok*. This is where he rose to prominence and gained the attention from the likes of Elton John, Alicia Keys, Justin Bieber and Sia. By the end of the year he was the most followed artist on the *Tik Tok* platform.

He signed up to Parlophone and his debut EP gained over 100 million global streams. A sold-out tour followed.

Space Man was written during the lockdown and was sent to the BBC whereby he was the chosen artist for Eurovision.

Before the final, the song was critically acclaimed not only by the UK media but by the European media as well. It was perceived to be a possible winner of the competition and favoured among the bookmakers.

He performed in the final in twenty-second position and finished in a superb second place with 466 points, he became the highest scoring UK Eurovision entrant and scored the UK's best result since 1998. It was also the sixteenth time the UK had finished runner's up.

As for the single release it peaked at number two in the UK singles chart and had over forty-five million streams on Spotify.

One of the legacies of Ryder's *Space man* seems to be that the feelgood factor for the UK in Eurovision has come back. There is definitely a more positive attitude towards Eurovision in the mainstream British media. Long may it continue.

There were also over 161 million viewers for Eurovision this year. Not only traditional television viewing but the internet viewing phenomenon has really taken off.

Author's Comment:
Absolutely fantastic, totally different from the run of the mill entries we have been churning out the last few years. It put the spark back and seemed to lift the spirits of the long-suffering UK Eurovision audience. Long may it continue.

The 2020s

The UK has finally escaped its nul points nightmare

With Sam Ryder's second, our Eurovision luck changed for the better after some terrible flops, writes **Charlotte Cripps**

Guitar hero: Ryder finished behind Ukraine in Turin (AFP/Getty)

"It's great to see you guys trying for once!" This was the general consensus backstage in the press area at the Eurovision Song Contest this year, where the UK entry, singer-songwriter and Tik Tok star Sam Ryder, came second place with his song "Space Man".

Our music editor was stationed in Turin, Italy, for the contest at the city's 2006 Winter Olympics venue, the Pala Alpitour – also known as the PalaOlimpico – where she was live blogging the event. After the voting was done and dusted, there was great excitement as war-torn Ukraine won the contest with Kalush Orchestra's song "Stefania".

Now that Ryder is a UK Eurovision hero, it has proved once and for all that our spectacular run of flops – in 2021 we achieved "nul points" with James Newman's "Embers" – hasn't been because of Brexit or Europe's dislike of the UK. It's simply because we haven't entered anything good enough.

We used to act like Eurovision was uncool and cheesy in the Nineties but changing attitudes are why we did so well this year, we actually sent a good singer with proper live performance credentials

The Independent, May 21st, 2022

The UK in Eurovision - *The Highs and Lows*

2023

Mai Muller

Due to the ongoing war in the Ukraine it is deemed unsafe for them to host the event after Kalush Orchestra's winning song *Stefania*.

The UK finished in second place so hence after twenty-five years the UK gets to host the competition once more, in the city of Liverpool.

Unfortunately Eurovision is being held during the dates of 9th, 11th and 13th May and this book will have gone to press before we know the outcome.

We do however know the representative, a one Mai Muller with a song called *I Wrote a Song*.

Mai Muller is a 25-year-old singer, songwriter, and the song was co-written with Lewis Thompson and Karen Poole. Poole incidentally has written for the likes of Kylie Minogue and David Guetta and was founding member of the 90's pop duo Alisha's Attic. So the song has a catchy dance beat, with lyrics about revenge on an ex-boyfriend.

The knives are already out on the entry. *The Guardian* newspaper already compared the song to Sam Ryder's brilliant *Space man*. They seem to think the powers that be have reverted back to the safe current pop trends of now, rather than something out of the ordinary like *Space man* which seemed to capture everybody's imagination.

We shall see. In a few weeks we will know if they have picked a winner or not. I was going to put my neck on the line and say, I don't believe she stands a chance of winning. There is a certain Eurovision superstar representing Sweden again this year, that was where my money was going. Having heard Mai's song several times the more I like it. It is catchy, also the unofficial Eurovision blog sites are going crazy for it. I now believe she stands a good chance of at least a top five if not the winner.

Watch this Space!

GOOD LUCK MAI!

*So there we have it folks,
the 2010s-2023 and the end of the story so far.
Not a great twelve years, only one standout
second place entry to shout about —
Sam Ryder's* Space man.
*We even had a couple of old music superstars
representing us. They still failed to produce a
winning entry — a song that was capable of
running close would have been nice.
I'm not going to criticise the artists, but I will
point the finger at the powers that be that pick
the entries and songs to put in front of the
public.
It needs shaking up.
2022 was an exception they got right.
I am not so sure with 2023, but I could be
wrong. I hope so!
Anyway, it has been a blast researching this
book and I hope you enjoy reading it as much
as I have writing it.*

Good luck Liverpool!

All the UK entrants at a glance

1956 *Non participation*
1957 Patricia Bredin
1958 *Non participation*
1959 Pearl Lavinia Carr and Edward Victor Johnson
1960 Bryan Johnson
1961 The Allisons
1962 Ronnie Carroll
1963 Ronnie Carroll
1964 Matt Monroe
1965 Kathy Kirby
1966 Kenneth McKeller
1967 Sandie Shaw
1968 Cliff Richard
1969 Lulu
1970 Mary Hopkin
1971 Clodagh Rogers
1972 The New Seekers
1973 Cliff Richard
1974 Olivia Newton-John
1975 The Shadows
1976 Brotherhood of Man
1977 Lynsey DePaul & Mike Moran
1978 CoCo
1979 Black Lace
1980 Prima Donna
1981 Bucks Fizz
1982 Bardo
1983 Sweet Dreams
1984 Belle and the Devotions
1985 Vikki
1986 Ryder
1987 Rikki
1988 Scott Fitzgerald
1989 Live Report
1990 Emma
1991 Samantha Janus
1992 Michael Ball
1993 Sonia
1994 Francis Ruffelle
1995 Love City Grove
1996 Gina G
1997 Katrina and the Waves
1998 Imaani
1999 Precious
2000 Nikki French
2001 Lindsay Dracass
2002 Jessica Garlick
2003 Jemini
2004 James Fox
2005 Javine
2006 Daz Sampson
2007 Scooch
2008 Andy Abraham
2009 Jade Ewen
2010 Josh Dubovie
2011 Blue
2012 Engelbert Humperdinck
2013 Bonnie Tyler
2014 Molly
2015 Electric Velvet
2016 Joe and Jake
2017 Lucie Jones
2018 SuRie
2019 Michael Rice
2020 *COVID-19 Pandemic*
2021 James Newman
2022 Sam Ryder
2023 Mai Muller

Result scoreboards from 1956 to present day

**From 2004 semi-finals were introduced to accommodate all the countries that wanted to take part.
These semi-finals are not included in these following result pages.**

1956

POSITION	COUNTRY	SONG	ARTIST	POINTS
1	Switzerland	Refrain	Lys Assia	–
2	Netherlands	De Vogels Van Holland	Jetty Paerl	–
2	Switzerland	Das Alte Karussell	Lys Assia	–
2	Belgium	Messieurs Les Noyés De La Seine	Fud Leclerc	–
2	Germany	Im Wartesaal Zum Großen Glück	Walter Andreas Schwarz	–
2	France	Le Temps Perdu	Mathé Altéry	–
2	Luxembourg	Ne Crois Pas	Michèle Arnaud	–
2	Italy	Aprite Le Finestre	Franca Raimondi	–
2	Netherlands	Voorgoed Voorbij	Corry Brokken	–
2	Belgium	Le Plus Beau Jour De Ma Vie	Mony Marc	–
2	Germany	So Geht Das Jede Nacht	Freddy Quinn	–
2	France	Il Est Là	Dany Dauberson	–
2	Luxembourg	Les Amants De Minuit	Michèle Arnaud	–
2	Italy	Amami Se Vuoi	Tonina Torielli	–

1957

POSITION	COUNTRY	SONG	ARTIST	POINTS
1	Netherlands	Net Als Toen	Corry Brokken	31
2	France	La Belle Amour	Paule Desjardins	17
3	Denmark	Skibet Skal Sejle I Nat	Birthe Wilke & Gustav Winckler	10
4	Luxembourg	Amours Mortes (Tant De Peine)	Danièle Dupré	8
4	Germany	Telefon, Telefon	Margot Hielscher	8
6	Italy	Corde Della Mia Chitarra	Nunzio Gallo	7
7	**United Kingdom**	**All**	**Patricia Bredin**	**6**
8	Belgium	Straatdeuntje	Bobbejaan Schoepen	5
8	Switzerland	L'enfant Que J'étais	Lys Assia	5
10	Austria	Wohin, Kleines Pony	Bob Martin	3

1958

POSITION	COUNTRY	SONG	ARTIST	POINTS
1	France	Dors Mon Amour	André Claveau	27
2	Switzerland	Giorgio	Lys Assia	24
3	Italy	Nel Blu Dipinto Di Blu	Domenico Modugno	13
4	Sweden	Lilla Stjärna	Alice Babs	10
5	Belgium	Ma Petite Chatte	Fud Leclerc	8
5	Austria	Die Ganze Welt Braucht Liebe	Liane Augustin	8
7	Germany	Für Zwei Groschen Musik	Margot Hielscher	5
8	Denmark	Jeg Rev Et Blad Ud Af Min Dagbog	Raquel Rastenni	3
9	Netherlands	Heel De Wereld	Corry Brokken	1
9	Luxembourg	Un Grand Amour	Solange Berry	1

1959

POSITION	COUNTRY	SONG	ARTIST	POINTS
1	Netherlands	Een Beetje	Teddy Scholten	21
2	**United Kingdom**	**Sing Little Birdie**	**Pearl Carr & Teddy Johnson**	**16**
3	France	Oui, Oui, Oui, Oui	Jean Philippe	15
4	Switzerland	Irgendwoher	Christa Williams	14
5	Denmark	Uh, Jeg Ville Ønske Jeg Var Dig	Birthe Wilke	12
6	Italy	Piove	Domenico Modugno	9
6	Belgium	Hou Toch Van Mij	Bob Benny	9
8	Germany	Heut' Woll'n Wir Tanzen Geh'n	Alice and Ellen Kessler	5
9	Sweden	Augustin	Brita Borg	4
9	Austria	Der K. Und K. Kalypso Aus Wien	Ferry Graf	4
11	Monaco	Mon Ami Pierrot	Jacques Pills	1

The UK in Eurovision - *The Highs and Lows*

1960

POSITION	COUNTRY	SONG	ARTIST	POINTS
1	France	Tom Pillibi	Jacqueline Boyer	32
2	**United Kingdom**	**Looking High, High, High**	**Bryan Johnson**	**25**
3	Monaco	Ce Soir-là	François Deguelt	15
4	Norway	Voi-voi	Nora Brockstedt	11
4	Germany	Bonne Nuit, Ma Chérie!	Wyn Hoop	11
6	Belgium	Mon Amour Pour Toi	Fud Leclerc	9
7	Austria	Du Hast Mich So Fasziniert	Harry Winter	6
8	Switzerland	Cielo E Terra	Anita Traversi	5
8	Italy	Romantica	Renato Rascel	5
10	Sweden	Alla Andra Får Varann	Siw Malmkvist	4
10	Denmark	Det Var En Yndig Tid	Katy Bødtger	4
12	Netherlands	Wat Een Geluk	Rudi Carrell	2
13	Luxembourg	So Laang We's Du Do Bast	Camillo Felgen	1

1961

POSITION	COUNTRY	SONG	ARTIST	POINTS
1	Luxembourg	Nous Les Amoureux	Jean-Claude Pascal	31
2	**United Kingdom**	**Are You Sure?**	**The Allisons**	**24**
3	Switzerland	Nous Aurons Demain	Franca di Rienzo	16
4	France	Printemps (avril Carillonne)	Jean-Paul Mauric	13
5	Denmark	Angelique	Dario Campeotto	12
5	Italy	Al Di Là	Betty Curtis	12
7	Norway	Sommer i Palma	Nora Brockstedt	10
8	Yugoslavia	Neke Davne Zvezde	Ljiljana Petrović	9
9	Spain	Estando Contigo	Conchita Bautista	8
10	Monaco	Allons, Allons Les Enfants	Colette Deréal	6
10	Finland	Valoa Ikkunassa	Laila Kinnunen	6
10	Netherlands	Wat Een Dag	Greetje Kauffeld	6
13	Germany	Einmal Sehen Wir Uns Wieder	Lale Andersen	3
14	Sweden	April, April	Lill-Babs	2
15	Austria	Sehnsucht	Jimmy Makulis	1
15	Belgium	September, Gouden Roos	Bob Benny	1

1962

POSITION	COUNTRY	SONG	ARTIST	POINTS
1	France	Un Premier Amour	Isabelle Aubret	26
2	Monaco	Dis Rien	François Deguelt	13
3	Luxembourg	Petit Bonhomme	Camillo Felgen	11
4	Yugoslavia	Ne Pali Svetlo U Sumrak	Lola Novaković	10
4	**United Kingdom**	**Ring-a-ding Girl**	**Ronnie Carroll**	**10**
6	Germany	Zwei Kleine Italiener	Conny Froboess	9
7	Finland	Tipi-tii	Marion Rung	4
7	Sweden	Sol Och Vår	Inger Berggren	4
9	Italy	Addio, Addio	Claudio Villa	3
10	Denmark	Vuggevise	Ellen Winther	2
10	Norway	Kom Sol, Kom Regn	Inger Jacobsen	2
10	Switzerland	Le Retour	Jean Philippe	2
13	Belgium	Ton Nom	Fud Leclerc	0
13	Spain	Llámame	Victor Balaguer	0
13	Austria	Nur In Der Wiener Luft	Eleonore Schwarz	0
13	Netherlands	Katinka	De Spelbrekers	0

1963

POSITION	COUNTRY	SONG	ARTIST	POINTS
1	Denmark	Dansevise	Grethe & Jørgen Ingmann	42
2	Switzerland	T'en Va Pas	Esther Ofarim	40
3	Italy	Uno Per Tutte	Emilio Pericoli	37
4	**United Kingdom**	**Say Wonderful Things**	**Ronnie Carroll**	**28**
5	France	Elle était Si Jolie	Alain Barrière	25
5	Monaco	L'amour S'en Va	Françoise Hardy	25
7	Austria	Vielleicht Geschieht Ein Wunder	Carmela Corren	16
8	Luxembourg	A Force De Prier	Nana Mouskouri	13
9	Germany	Marcel	Heidi Brühl	5
10	Belgium	Waarom	Jacques Raymond	4
11	Yugoslavia	Brodovi	Vice Vukov	3
12	Spain	Algo Prodigioso	José Guardiola	2
13	Netherlands	Een Speeldoos	Annie Palmen	0
13	Norway	Solhverv	Anita Thallaug	0
13	Finland	Muistojeni Laulu	Laila Halme	0
13	Sweden	En Gång I Stockholm	Monica Zetterlund	0

1964

POSITION	COUNTRY	SONG	ARTIST	POINTS
1	Italy	Non Ho L'età	Gigliola Cinquetti	49
2	**United Kingdom**	**I Love The Little Things**	**Matt Monro**	**17**
3	Monaco	Où Sont-elles Passées?	Romuald	15
4	Luxembourg	Dès Que Le Printemps Revient	Hugues Aufray	14
4	France	Le Chant De Mallory	Rachel	14
6	Austria	Warum Nur, Warum?	Udo Jürgens	11
7	Finland	Laiskotellen	Lasse Mårtenson	9
8	Norway	Spiral	Arne Bendiksen	6
9	Denmark	Sangen Om Dig	Bjørn Tidmand	4
10	Netherlands	Jij Bent Mijn Leven	Anneke Grönloh	2
10	Belgium	Près De Ma Rivière	Robert Cogoi	2
12	Spain	Caracola	Tim, Nelly and Tony	1
13	Germany	Man Gewöhnt Sich So Schnell An Das Schöne	Nora Nova	0
13	Portugal	Oração	António Calvário	0
13	Yugoslavia	Život je sklopio krug	Sabahudin Kurt	0
13	Switzerland	I Miei Pensieri	Anita Traversi	0

The UK in Eurovision - *The Highs and Lows*

1965

POSITION	COUNTRY	SONG	ARTIST	POINTS
2	**United Kingdom**	**I Belong**	**Kathy Kirby**	**26**
3	France	N'avoue Jamais	Guy Mardel	22
4	Austria	Sag Ihr, Ich Lass' Sie Grüßen	Udo Jürgens	16
5	Italy	Se Piangi, Se Ridi	Bobby Solo	15
6	Ireland	I'm Walking The Streets In The Rain	Butch Moore	11
7	Denmark	For Din Skyld	Birgit Brüel	10
8	Switzerland	Non à Jamais Sans Toi	Yovanna	8
9	Monaco	Va Dire à L'amour	Marjorie Noël	7
10	Sweden	Absent Friend	Ingvar Wixell	6
11	Netherlands	Het Is Genoeg	Conny Van den bos	5
12	Yugoslavia	Ceznja	Vice Vukov	2
13	Norway	Karusell	Kirsti Sparboe	1
13	Portugal	Sol De Inverno	Simone de Oliveira	1
15	Spain	Qué Bueno, Qué Bueno	Conchita Bautista	0
15	Germany	Paradies, Wo Bist Du?	Ulla Wiesner	0
15	Belgium	Als Het Weer Lente Is	Lize Marke	0
15	Finland	Aurinko Laskee Länteen	Viktor Klimenko	0

1966

POSITION	COUNTRY	SONG	ARTIST	POINTS
1	Austria	Merci Chérie	Udo Jürgens	31
2	Sweden	Nygammal Vals	Lill Lindfors & Svante Thuresson	16
3	Norway	Intet Er Nytt Under Solen	Åse Kleveland	15
4	Belgium	Un Peu De Poivre, Un Peu De Sel	Tonia	14
4	Ireland	Come Back To Stay	Dickie Rock	14
6	Switzerland	Ne Vois-tu Pas?	Madeleine Pascal	12
7	Yugoslavia	Brez Besed	Berta Ambroz	9
7	Spain	Yo Soy Aquél	Raphael	9
9	**United Kingdom**	**A Man Without Love**	**Kenneth McKellar**	**8**
10	Germany	Die Zeiger Der Uhr	Margot Eskens	7
10	Luxembourg	Ce Soir Je T'attendais	Michèle Torr	7
10	Finland	Play-boy	Ann-Christine Nyström	7
13	Portugal	Ele E Ela	Madalena Iglesias	6
14	Denmark	Stop mens legen er go'	Ulla Pia	4
15	Netherlands	Fernando En Philippo	Milly Scott	2
16	France	Chez Nous	Dominique Walter	1
17	Monaco	Bien Plus Fort	Tereza	0
17	Italy	Dio Come Ti Amo	Domenico Modugno	0

1967

POSITION	COUNTRY	SONG	ARTIST	POINTS
1	United Kingdom	Puppet On A String	Sandie Shaw	47
2	Ireland	If I Could Choose	Sean Dunphy	22
3	France	Il Doit Faire Beau Là-bas	Noëlle Cordier	20
4	Luxembourg	L'amour Est Bleu	Vicky	17
5	Monaco	Boum-badaboum	Minouche Barelli	10
6	Spain	Hablemos Del Amor	Raphael	9
7	Belgium	Ik Heb Zorgen	Louis Neefs	8
8	Sweden	Som En Dröm	Östen Warnerbring	7
8	Germany	Anouschka	Inge Brück	7
8	Yugoslavia	Vse Rože Sveta	Lado Leskovar	7
11	Italy	Non Andare Più Lontano	Claudio Villa	4
12	Portugal	O Vento Mudou	Eduardo Nascimento	3
12	Finland	Varjoon-suojaan	Fredi	3
14	Netherlands	Ring-dinge	Thérèse Steinmetz	2
14	Austria	Warum Es Hunderttausend Sterne Gibt	Peter Horten	2
14	Norway	Dukkemann	Kirsti Sparboe	2
17	Switzerland	Quel Cœur Vas-tu Briser?	Géraldine	0

1968

POSITION	COUNTRY	SONG	ARTIST	POINTS
1	Spain	La, La, La...	Massiel	29
2	United Kingdom	Congratulations	Cliff Richard	28
3	France	La Source	Isabelle Aubret	20
4	Ireland	Chance Of A Lifetime	Pat McGeegan	18
5	Sweden	Det Börjar Verka Kärlek, Banne Mej	Claes-Göran Hederström	15
6	Germany	Ein Hoch Der Liebe	Wencke Myhre	11
7	Belgium	Quand Tu Reviendras	Claude Lombard	8
7	Monaco	A Chacun Sa Chanson	Line & Willy	8
7	Yugoslavia	Jedan Dan	Luci Kapurso & Hamo Hajdarhodzic	8
10	Italy	Marianne	Sergio Endrigo	7
11	Portugal	Verão	Carlos Mendes	5
11	Luxembourg	Nous Vivrons D'amour	Chris Baldo & Sophie Garel	5
13	Austria	Tausend Fenster	Karel Gott	2
13	Switzerland	Guardando Il Sole	Gianni Mascolo	2
13	Norway	Stress	Odd Børre	2
16	Netherlands	Morgen	Ronnie Tober	1
16	Finland	Kun Kello Käy	Kristina Hautala	1

1969

POSITION	COUNTRY	SONG	ARTIST	POINTS
1	Spain	Vivo Cantando	Salomé	18
1	United Kingdom	Boom Bang-a-bang	Lulu	18
1	Netherlands	De Troubadour	Lenny Kuhr	18
1	France	Un Jour, Un Enfant	Frida Boccara	18
5	Switzerland	Bonjour, Bonjour	Paola del Medico	13
6	Monaco	Maman, Maman	Jean-Jacques	11
7	Ireland	The Wages Of Love	Muriel Day and the Lindsays	10
7	Belgium	Jennifer Jennings	Louis Neefs	10
9	Sweden	Judy, Min Vän	Tommy Körberg	8
9	Germany	Primaballerina	Siw Malmkvist	8
11	Luxembourg	Cathérine	Romuald	7
12	Finland	Kuin Silloin Ennen	Jarkko & Laura	6
13	Yugoslavia	Pozdrav Svijetu	Ivan & M's	5
13	Italy	Due Grosse Lacrime Bianche	Iva Zanicchi	5
15	Portugal	Desfolhada Portuguesa	Simone de Oliveira	4
16	Norway	Oj, Oj, Oj, Så Glad, Jeg Skal Bli	Kirsti Sparboe	1

The UK in Eurovision - *The Highs and Lows*

1970

POSITION	COUNTRY	SONG	ARTIST	POINTS
1	Ireland	All Kinds Of Everything	Dana	32
2	**United Kingdom**	**Knock, Knock (who's there?)**	**Mary Hopkin**	**26**
3	Germany	Wunder Gibt Es Immer Wieder	Katja Ebstein	12
4	Switzerland	Retour	Henri Dès	8
4	France	Marie Blanche	Guy Bonnet	8
4	Spain	Gwendolyne	Julio Iglesias	8
7	Netherlands	Waterman	Patricia & Hearts of Soul	7
8	Italy	Occhi Di Ragazza	Gianni Morandi	5
8	Belgium	Viens L'oublier	Jean Vallée	5
8	Monaco	Marlène	Dominique Dussault	5
11	Yugoslavia	Pridi, Dala Ti Bom Cvet	Eva Sršen	4
12	Luxembourg	Je Suis Tombé Du Ciel	David-Alexandre Winter	0

1971

POSITION	COUNTRY	SONG	ARTIST	POINTS
1	Monaco	Un Banc, Un Arbre, Une Rue	Séverine	128
2	Spain	En Un Mundo Nuevo	Karina	116
3	Germany	Diese Welt	Katja Ebstein	100
4	**United Kingdom**	**Jack In The Box**	**Clodagh Rodgers**	**98**
5	Italy	L'amore è Un Attimo	Massimo Ranieri	91
6	Sweden	Vita Vidder	Family Four	85
6	Netherlands	De Tijd	Saskia and Serge	85
8	Finland	Tie Uuteen Päivään	Markku Aro and Koivisto Sisters	84
9	Portugal	Menina Do Alto Da Serra	Tonicha	83
10	France	Un Jardin Sur La Terre	Serge Lama	82
11	Ireland	One Day Love	Angela Farrell	79
12	Switzerland	Les Illusions De Nos Vingt Ans	Peter, Sue and Marc	78
13	Luxembourg	Pomme, Pomme, Pomme	Monique Melsen	70
14	Belgium	Goeie Morgen, Morgen	Lily Castel and Jacques Raymond	68
14	Yugoslavia	Tvoj Djecak Je Tuzan	Krunoslav Slabinac	68
16	Austria	Musik	Marianne Mendt	66
17	Norway	Lykken Er...	Hanne Krogh	65
18	Malta	Marija L-Maltija	Joe Grech	52

1972

POSITION	COUNTRY	SONG	ARTIST	POINTS
1	Luxembourg	Après Toi	Vicky Leandros	128
2	**United Kingdom**	**Beg, Steal or Borrow**	**The New Seekers**	**114**
3	Germany	Nur Die Liebe Läßt Uns Leben	Mary Roos	107
4	Netherlands	Als Het Om De Liefde Gaat	Sandra & Andres	106
5	Austria	Falter Im Wind	The Milestones	100
6	Italy	I Giorni Dell' Arcobaleno	Nicola di Bari	92
7	Portugal	A Festa Da Vida	Carlos Mendes	90
8	Switzerland	C'est La Chanson De Mon Amour	Véronique Müller	88
9	Yugoslavia	Muzika I Ti	Tereza	87
10	Spain	Amanece	Jaime Morey	83
11	France	Comé-comédie	Betty Mars	81
12	Finland	Muistathan	Päivi Paunu and Kim Floor	78
13	Sweden	Härliga Sommardag	Family Four	75
14	Norway	Småting	Grethe Kausland & Benny Borg	73
15	Ireland	Ceol On Ghrá	Sandie Jones	72
16	Monaco	Comme On S'aime	Anne-Marie Godart and Peter MacLane	65
17	Belgium	À La Folie Ou Pas Du Tout	Serge and Christine Ghisoland	55
18	Malta	L-imħabba	Helen & Joseph	48

1973

POSITION	COUNTRY	SONG	ARTIST	POINTS
1	Luxembourg	Tu Te Reconnaîtras	Anne-Marie David	129
2	Spain	Eres Tú	Mocedades	125
3	**United Kingdom**	**Power To All Our Friends**	**Cliff Richard**	**123**
4	Israel	Ey-sham	Ilanit	97
5	Sweden	You're Summer	The Nova and The Dolls	94
6	Finland	Tom Tom Tom	Marion Rung	93
7	Norway	It's Just A Game	Bendik Singers	89
8	Germany	Junger Tag	Gitte	85
8	Monaco	Un Train Qui Part	Marie	85
10	Portugal	Tourada	Fernando Tordo	80
10	Ireland	Do I Dream?	Maxi	80
12	Switzerland	Je vais me marier, Marie	Patrick Juvet	79
13	Italy	Chi Sarà Con Te	Massimo Ranieri	74
14	Netherlands	De Oude Muzikant	Ben Cramer	69
15	Yugoslavia	Gori Vatra	Zdravko Colic	65
15	France	Sans Toi	Martine Clémenceau	65
17	Belgium	Baby, Baby	Nicole and Hugo	58

1974

POSITION	COUNTRY	SONG	ARTIST	POINTS
1	Sweden	Waterloo	ABBA	24
2	Italy	Si	Gigliola Cinquetti	18
3	Netherlands	I See A Star	Mouth & MacNeal	15
4	**United Kingdom**	**Long Live Love**	**Olivia Newton-John**	**14**
4	Luxembourg	Bye, Bye, I Love You	Ireen Sheer	14
4	Monaco	Celui Qui Reste Et Celui Qui S'en Va	Romuald	14
7	Israel	Natati La Khayay	Kaveret (Poogy)	11
7	Ireland	Cross Your Heart	Tina	11
9	Spain	Canta Y Se Feliz	Peret	10
9	Belgium	Fleur De Liberté	Jacques Hustin	10
11	Greece	Krassi, Thalassa Ke T'agori Mou	Marinella	7
12	Yugoslavia	Moja Generacija	Korni	6
13	Finland	Äla Mene Pois (keep Me Warm)	Carita	4
14	Norway	The First Day Of Love	Anne-Karine Ström and the Bendik Singers	3
14	Germany	Die Sommermelodie	Cindy und Bert	3
14	Switzerland	Mein Ruf Nach Dir	Piera Martell	3
14	Portugal	E Depois Do Adeus	Paulo de Carvalho	3

The UK in Eurovision - *The Highs and Lows*

1975

POSITION	COUNTRY	SONG	ARTIST	POINTS
1	Netherlands	Ding-A-Dong	Teach-In	152
2	**United Kingdom**	**Let Me Be The One**	**The Shadows**	**138**
3	Italy	Era	Wess & Dori Ghezzi	115
4	France	Et Bonjour à Toi L'artiste	Nicole Rieu	91
5	Luxembourg	Toi	Géraldine	84
6	Switzerland	Mikado	Simone Drexel	77
7	Finland	Old Man Fiddle	Pihasoittajat	74
8	Sweden	Jennie, Jennie	Lars Berghagen and the Dolls	72
9	Ireland	That's What Friends Are For	The Swarbriggs	68
10	Spain	Tú Volverás	Sergio & Estíbaliz	53
11	Israel	At Va'Ani	Shlomo Artzi	40
12	Malta	Singing This Song	Renato	32
13	Yugoslavia	Dan Ljubezni	Pepel In Kri	22
13	Monaco	Une Chanson C'est Une Lettre	Sophie	22
15	Belgium	Gelukkig Zijn	Ann Christy	17
16	Portugal	Madrugada	Duarte Mendes	16
17	Germany	Ein Lied Kann Eine Brücke Sein	Joy Fleming	15
18	Norway	You Touched My Life With Summer	Ellen Nikolaysen	11
19	Turkey	Seninle Bir Dakika	Semiha Yankı	3

1976

POSITION	COUNTRY	SONG	ARTIST	POINTS
1	**United Kingdom**	**Save Your Kisses For Me**	**Brotherhood of Man**	**164**
2	France	Un, Deux, Trois	Catherine Ferry	147
3	Monaco	Toi, La Musique Et Moi	Mary Christy	93
4	Switzerland	Djambo, Djambo	Peter, Sue & Marc	91
5	Austria	My Little World	Waterloo & Robinson	80
6	Israel	Emor Shalom	Chocolate, Menta, Mastik	77
7	Italy	We'll Live It All Again	Romina and Al Bano	69
8	Belgium	Judy Et Cie	Pierre Rapsat	68
9	Netherlands	The Party's Over Now	Sandra Reemer	56
10	Ireland	When	Red Hurley	54
11	Finland	Pump-pump	Fredi and The Friends	44
12	Portugal	Uma Flor De Verde Pinho	Carlos do Carmo	24
13	Greece	Panaghia Mou, Panaghia Mou	Mariza Koch	20
14	Luxembourg	Chansons Pour Ceux Qui S'aiment	Jürgen Marcus	17
15	Germany	Sing, Sang, Song	Les Humphries Singers	12
16	Spain	Sobran Las Palabras	Braulio	11
17	Yugoslavia	Ne Mogu Skriti Svoju Bol	Ambasadori	10
18	Norway	Mata Hari	Anne-Karine Ström	7

1977

POSITION	COUNTRY	SONG	ARTIST	POINTS
1	France	L'oiseau Et L'enfant	Marie Myriam	136
2	**United Kingdom**	**Rock Bottom**	**Lynsey de Paul & Mike Moran**	**121**
3	Ireland	It's Nice To Be In Love Again	The Swarbriggs Plus Two	119
4	Monaco	Une Petite Française	Michèle Torr	96
5	Greece	Mathima Solfez	Pascalis, Marianna, Robert and Bessy	92
6	Switzerland	Swiss Lady	Pepe Lienhard Band	71
7	Belgium	A Million In One, Two, Three	Dream Express	69
8	Germany	Telegram	Silver Convention	55
9	Spain	Enseñame A Cantar	Micky	52
10	Finland	Lapponia	Monica Aspelund	50
11	Israel	Ah-haa-vah Hee Shir Lish-naa-yim	Ilanit	49
12	Netherlands	De Mallemolen	Heddy Lester	35
13	Italy	Liberà	Mia Martini	33
14	Norway	Casanova	Anita Skorgan	18
14	Portugal	Portugal No Coração	Os Amigos	18
16	Luxembourg	Frère Jacques	Anne Marie B.	17
17	Austria	Boom Boom Boomerang	Schmetterlinge	11
18	Sweden	Beatles	Forbes	2

1978

POSITION	COUNTRY	SONG	ARTIST	POINTS
1	Israel	A-Ba-Ni-Bi	Izhar Cohen and the Alphabeta	157
2	Belgium	L'amour ça Fait Chanter La Vie	Jean Vallée	125
3	France	Il Y Aura Toujours Des Violons	Joël Prévost	119
4	Monaco	Les Jardins De Monaco	Caline and Olivier Toussaint	107
5	Ireland	Born To Sing	Colm T. Wilkinson	86
6	Germany	Feuer	Ireen Sheer	84
7	Luxembourg	Parlez-vous Français?	Baccara	73
8	Greece	Charlie Chaplin	Tania Tsanaklidou	66
9	Spain	Bailemos Un Vals	José Vélez	65
9	Switzerland	Vivre	Carole Vinci	65
11	**United Kingdom**	**The Bad Old Days**	**Co-Co**	**61**
12	Italy	Questo Amore	Ricchi e Poveri	53
13	Netherlands	't Is Ok	Harmony	37
14	Sweden	Det Blir Alltid Värre Framåt Natten	Björn Skifs	26
15	Austria	Mrs. Caroline Robinson	Springtime	14
16	Denmark	Boom Boom	Mabel	13
17	Portugal	Dai-li-dou	Gemini	5
18	Finland	Anna Rakkaudelle Tilaisuus	Seija Simola	2
18	Turkey	Sevince	Nazar	2
20	Norway	Mil Etter Mil	Jahn Teigen	0

The UK in Eurovision - *The Highs and Lows*

1979

POSITION	COUNTRY	SONG	ARTIST	POINTS
1	Israel	Hallelujah	Milk and Honey	125
2	Spain	Su Canción	Betty Missiego	116
3	France	Je Suis L'enfant-soleil	Anne-Marie David	106
4	Germany	Dschinghis Khan	Dschinghis Khan	86
5	Ireland	Happy Man	Cathal Dunne	80
6	Denmark	Disco Tango	Tommy Seebach	76
7	**United Kingdom**	**Mary Ann**	**Black Lace**	**73**
8	Greece	Socrati	Elpida	69
9	Portugal	Sobe, Sobe, Balão Sobe	Manuela Bravo	64
10	Switzerland	Trödler Und Co.	Peter, Sue & Marc & Pfuri, Gorps & Kniri	60
11	Norway	Oliver	Anita Skorgan	57
12	Netherlands	Colorado	Xandra	51
13	Luxembourg	J'ai Déjà Vu ça Dans Tes Yeux	Jeane Manson	44
14	Finland	Katson Sineen Taivaan	Katri-Helena	38
15	Italy	Raggio Di Luna	Matia Bazar	27
16	Monaco	Notre Vie, C'est La Musique	Laurent Vaguener	12
17	Sweden	Satellit	Ted Gärdestad	8
18	Belgium	Hey Nana	Micha Marah	5
18	Austria	Heute In Jerusalem	Christina Simon	5

1980

POSITION	COUNTRY	SONG	ARTIST	POINTS
1	Ireland	What's Another Year	Johnny Logan	143
2	Germany	Theater	Katja Ebstein	128
3	**United Kingdom**	**Love Enough For Two**	**Prima Donna**	**106**
4	Switzerland	Cinéma	Paola	104
5	Netherlands	Amsterdam	Maggie MacNeal	93
6	Italy	Non So Che Darei	Alan Sorrenti	87
7	Portugal	Um Grande, Grande Amor	José Cid	71
8	Austria	Du Bist Musik	Blue Danube	64
9	Luxembourg	Papa Pingouin	Sophie and Magaly	56
10	Sweden	Just Nu!	Tomas Ledin	47
11	France	Hé, Hé M'sieurs Dames	Profil	45
12	Spain	Quédate Esta Noche	Trigo Limpio	38
13	Greece	Otostop	Anna Vissi and the Epikouri	30
14	Denmark	Tænker Altid På Dig	Bamses Venner	25
15	Turkey	Petr'oil	Ajda Pekkan	23
16	Norway	Sámiid Ædnan	Sverre Kjellsberg & Mattis Hætta	15
17	Belgium	Euro-vision	Telex	14
18	Morocco	Bitaqat Hub	Samira Bensaïd	7
19	Finland	Huilumies	Vesa-Matti Loiri	6

1981

POSITION	COUNTRY	SONG	ARTIST	POINTS
1	United Kingdom	Making Your Mind Up	Bucks Fizz	136
2	Germany	Johnny Blue	Lena Valaitis	132
3	France	Humanahum	Jean Gabilou	125
4	Switzerland	Io Senza Tei	Peter, Sue & Marc	121
5	Ireland	Horoscopes	Sheeba	105
6	Cyprus	Monika	Island	69
7	Israel	Halaylah	Habibi	56
8	Greece	Feggari Kalokerino	Yiannis Dimitras	55
9	Netherlands	Het Is Een Wonder	Linda Williams	51
10	Sweden	Fångad I En Dröm	Björn Skifs	50
11	Luxembourg	C'est Peut-être Pas L'Amérique	Jean-Claude Pascal	41
11	Denmark	Krøller Eller Ej	Debbie Cameron & Tommy Seebach	41
13	Belgium	Samson	Emly Starr	40
14	Spain	Y Solo Tú	Bacchelli	38
15	Yugoslavia	Leila	Seid-Memic Vajta	35
16	Finland	Reggae O.k.	Riki Sorsa	27
17	Austria	Wenn Du Da Bist	Marty Brem	20
18	Turkey	Dönme Dolap	Modern Folk Trio & Ayşegül	9
18	Portugal	Play-back	Carlos Paião	9
20	Norway	Aldri i Livet	Finn Kalvik	0

1982

POSITION	COUNTRY	SONG	ARTIST	POINTS
1	Germany	Ein Bißchen Frieden	Nicole	161
2	Israel	Hora	Avi Toledano	100
3	Switzerland	Amour On T'aime	Arlette Zola	97
4	Belgium	Si Tu Aimes Ma Musique	Stella	96
5	Cyprus	Mono I Agapi	Anna Vissi	85
6	Luxembourg	Cour Apres Le Temps	Svetlana	78
7	United Kingdom	One Step Further	Bardo	76
8	Sweden	Dag Efter Dag	Chips	67
9	Austria	Sonntag	Mess	57
10	Spain	Él	Lucía	52
11	Ireland	Here Today, Gone Tomorrow	The Duskeys	49
12	Norway	Adieu	Jahn Teigen & Anita Skorgan	40
13	Portugal	Bem-bom	Doce	32
14	Yugoslavia	Halo Halo	Aska	21
15	Turkey	Hani	Neco	20
16	Netherlands	Jij En Ik	Bill van Dijk	8
17	Denmark	Video-video	Brixx	5
18	Finland	Nuku Pommiin	Kojo	0

The UK in Eurovision - *The Highs and Lows*

1983

POSITION	COUNTRY	SONG	ARTIST	POINTS
1	Luxembourg	Si La Vie Est Cadeau	Corinne Hermès	142
2	Israel	Hi	Ofra Haza	136
3	Sweden	Främling	Carola Häggkvist	126
4	Yugoslavia	Dzuli	Danijel	125
5	Germany	Rücksicht	Hoffmann und Hoffmann	94
6	**United Kingdom**	**I'm Never Giving Up**	**Sweet Dreams**	**79**
7	Netherlands	Sing Me A Song	Bernadette	66
8	France	Vivre	Guy Bonnet	56
9	Norway	Do Re Mi	Jahn Teigen	53
9	Austria	Hurricane	Westend	53
11	Italy	Per Lucia	Riccardo Fogli	41
11	Finland	Fantasiaa	Ami Aspelund	41
13	Portugal	Esta Balada Que Te Dou	Armando Gama	33
14	Greece	Mou Les	Christie Stassinopoulou	32
15	Switzerland	Io Così Non Ci Sto	Mariella Farré	28
16	Cyprus	I Agapi Akoma Zi	Stavros and Constantina	26
17	Denmark	Kloden Drejer	Gry Johansen	16
18	Belgium	Rendez-vous	Pas de Deux	13
19	Turkey	Opera	Çetin Alp and the Short Wave	0
19	Spain	¿Quién Maneja Mi Barca?	Remedios Amaya	0

1984

POSITION	COUNTRY	SONG	ARTIST	POINTS
1	Sweden	Diggi-loo Diggy-ley	Herrey's	145
2	Ireland	Terminal '3'	Linda Martin	137
3	Spain	Lady, Lady	Bravo	106
4	Denmark	Det' Lige Det	Hot Eyes	101
5	Belgium	Avanti La Vie	Jacques Zegers	70
5	Italy	I Treni Di Tozeur	Alice & Battiato	70
7	**United Kingdom**	**Love Games**	**Belle and the Devotions**	**63**
8	France	Autant D'amoureux Que D'étoiles	Annick Thoumazeau	61
9	Finland	Hengaillaan	Kirka	46
10	Luxembourg	100% D'amour	Sophie Carle	39
11	Portugal	Silêncio E Tanta Gente	Maria Guinot	38
12	Turkey	Halay	Bes Yil Önce, On Yil Sonra	37
13	Netherlands	Ik Hou Van Jou	Maribelle	34
13	Germany	Aufrecht Geh'n	Mary Roos	34
15	Cyprus	Anna Maria Lena	Andy Paul	31
16	Switzerland	Welche Farbe Hat Der Sonnenschein	Rainy Day	30
17	Norway	Lenge Leve Livet	Dollie de Luxe	29
18	Yugoslavia	Ciao Amore	Vlado and Isolda	26
19	Austria	Einfach Weg	Anita	5

1985

POSITION	COUNTRY	SONG	ARTIST	POINTS
1	Norway	La Det Swinge	Bobbysocks	123
2	Germany	Für Alle	Wind	105
3	Sweden	Bra Vibrationer	Kikki Danielsson	103
4	**United Kingdom**	**Love Is...**	**Vikki**	**100**
5	Israel	Olé Olé	Izhar Cohen	93
6	Ireland	Wait Until The Weekend Comes	Maria Christian	91
7	Italy	Magic, Oh Magic	Al Bano and Romina Power	78
8	Austria	Kinder Dieser Welt	Gary Lux	60
9	Finland	Eläköön Elämä	Sonja Lumme	58
10	France	Femme Dans Ses Rêves Aussi	Roger Bens	56
11	Denmark	Sku' du spørg' fra no'en	Hot Eyes	41
12	Switzerland	Piano Piano	Mariella Farré & Pino Gasparini	39
13	Luxembourg	Children, Kinder, Enfants	Margo, Franck, Diane, Ireen, Malcolm & Chris	37
14	Spain	La Fiesta Terminó	Paloma San Basilio	36
14	Turkey	Di Dai Di Dai Dai (Aşık oldum)	MFÖ	36
16	Cyprus	To Katalava Arga	Lia Vishy	15
16	Greece	Miazoume	Takis Biniaris	15
18	Portugal	Penso Em Ti, Eu Sei	Adelaïde	9
19	Belgium	Laat Me Nu Gaan	Linda Lepomme	7

1986

POSITION	COUNTRY	SONG	ARTIST	POINTS
1	Belgium	J'aime La Vie	Sandra Kim	176
2	Switzerland	Pas Pour Moi	Daniela Simons	140
3	Luxembourg	L'amour De Ma Vie	Sherisse Laurence	117
4	Ireland	You Can Count On Me	Luv Bug	96
5	Sweden	E' De' Det Här Du Kallar Kärlek	Lasse Holm & Monica Törnell	78
6	Denmark	Du Er Fuld Af Løgn	Lise Haavik & Trax	77
7	**United Kingdom**	**Runner In The Night**	**Ryder**	**72**
8	Germany	Über Die Brücke Geh'n	Ingrid Peters	62
9	Turkey	Halley	Klips & Onlar	53
10	Spain	Valentino	Cadillac	51
11	Yugoslavia	Željo Moja	Doris Dragović	49
12	Norway	Romeo	Ketil Stokkan	44
13	Netherlands	Alles Heeft Ritme	Frizzle Sizzle	40
14	Portugal	Não Sejas Mau Para Mim	Dora	28
15	Finland	Päivä Kahden Ihmisen	Kari Kuivalainen	22
16	Iceland	Gleðibankinn	Icy	19
17	France	Européennes	Cocktail Chic	13
18	Austria	Die Zeit Ist Einsam	Timna Brauer	12
19	Israel	Yavoh Yom	Moti Galadi and Sarai Tzuriel	7
20	Cyprus	Tora Zo	Elpida	4

The UK in Eurovision - *The Highs and Lows*

1987

POSITION	COUNTRY	SONG	ARTIST	POINTS
1	Ireland	Hold Me Now	Johnny Logan	172
2	Germany	Laß Die Sonne In Dein Herz	Wind	141
3	Italy	Gente Di Mare	Umberto Tozzi and Raf	103
4	Yugoslavia	Ja Sam Za Ples	Novi Fosili	92
5	Netherlands	Rechtop In De Wind	Marcha	83
5	Denmark	En Lille Melodi	Anne-Cathrine Herdorf	83
7	Cyprus	Aspro Mavro	Alexia	80
8	Israel	Shir Habatlanim	Datner & Kushnir	73
9	Norway	Mitt Liv	Kate Gulbrandsen	65
10	Greece	Stop!	Bang	64
11	Belgium	Soldiers Of Love	Liliane Saint-Pierre	56
12	Sweden	Boogaloo	Lotta Engberg	50
13	**United Kingdom**	**Only The Light**	**Rikki**	**47**
14	France	Les Mots D'amour N'ont Pas De Dimanche	Christine Minier	44
15	Finland	Sata Salamaa	Vicky Rosti	32
16	Iceland	Hægt Og Hljótt	Halla Margarét	28
17	Switzerland	Moitié Moitié	Carole Rich	26
18	Portugal	Neste Barco à Vela	Nevada	15
19	Spain	No Estás Solo	Patricia Kraus	10
20	Austria	Nur Noch Gefühl	Gary Lux	8
21	Luxembourg	Amour Amour	Plastic Bertrand	4
22	Turkey	Şarkım sevgi üstüne	Seyyal Taner & Lokomotif	0

1988

POSITION	COUNTRY	SONG	ARTIST	POINTS
1	Switzerland	Ne Partez Pas Sans Moi	Céline Dion	137
2	**United Kingdom**	**Go**	**Scott Fitzgerald**	**136**
3	Denmark	Ka' Du Se Hva' Jeg Sa'	Kirsten & Søren	92
4	Luxembourg	Croire	Lara Fabian	90
5	Norway	For Vår Jord	Karoline Krüger	88
6	Yugoslavia	Mangup	Srebrna Krila	87
7	Israel	Ben Adam	Yardena Arazi	85
8	Ireland	Take Him Home	Jump the Gun	79
9	Netherlands	Shangri-la	Gerard Joling	70
10	France	Chanteur De Charme	Gérard Lenorman	64
11	Spain	La Chica Que Yo Quiero (made In Spain)	La Década	58
12	Sweden	Stad I Ljus	Tommy Körberg	52
12	Italy	Ti Scrivo	Luca Barbarossa	52
14	Germany	Lied Für Einen Freund	Maxi & Chris Garden	48
15	Turkey	Sufi	MFÖ	37
16	Iceland	Sókrates	Beathoven	20
17	Greece	Kloun	Aphroditi Fryda	10
18	Belgium	Laissez Briller Le Soleil	Reynaert	5
18	Portugal	Voltarei	Dora	5
20	Finland	Nauravat Silmät Muistetaan	Boulevard	3
21	Austria	Lisa Mona Lisa	Wilfried	0

1989

POSITION	COUNTRY	SONG	ARTIST	POINTS
1	Yugoslavia	Rock Me	Riva	137
2	**United Kingdom**	**Why Do I Always Get It Wrong**	**Live Report**	**130**
3	Denmark	Vi Maler Byen Rød	Birthe Kjær	111
4	Sweden	En Dag	Tommy Nilsson	110
5	Austria	Nur Ein Lied	Thomas Forstner	97
6	Spain	Nacida Para Amar	Nina	88
7	Finland	La Dolce Vita	Anneli Saaristo	76
8	France	J'ai Volé La Vie	Nathalie Pâque	60
9	Italy	Avrei Voluto	Anna Oxa & Fausto Leali	56
9	Greece	To Diko Sou Asteri	Marianna	56
11	Cyprus	Apopse As Vrethoume	Fanny Polymeri and Yiannis Savvidakis	51
12	Israel	Derech Ha'melech	Gili & Galit	50
13	Switzerland	Viver Senza Tei	Furbaz	47
14	Germany	Flieger	Nino de Angelo	46
15	Netherlands	Blijf Zoals Je Bent	Justine Pelmelay	45
16	Portugal	Conquistador	Da Vinci	39
17	Norway	Venners Nærhet	Britt Synnøve Johansen	30
18	Ireland	The Real Me	Kiev Connolly and the Missing Passengers	21
19	Belgium	Door De Wind	Ingeborg	13
20	Luxembourg	Monsieur	Park Café	8
21	Turkey	Bana Bana	Pan	5
22	Iceland	Það Sem Enginn Sér	Daníel Ágúst Haraldsson	0

1990

POSITION	COUNTRY	SONG	ARTIST	POINTS
1	Italy	Insieme: 1992	Toto Cutugno	149
2	France	White and Black Blues	Joelle Ursull	132
2	Ireland	Somewhere In Europe	Liam Reilly	132
4	Iceland	Eitt Lag Enn	Stjórnin	124
5	Spain	Bandido	Azúcar Moreno	96
6	**United Kingdom**	**Give A Little Love Back To The World**	**Emma**	**87**
7	Yugoslavia	Hajde Da Ludujemo	Tajci	81
8	Denmark	Hallo Hallo	Lonnie Devantier	64
9	Germany	Frei Zu Leben	Chris Kempers & Daniel Kovac	60
10	Austria	Keine Mauern Mehr	Simone	58
11	Switzerland	Musik Klingt In Die Welt Hinaus	Egon Egemann	51
12	Belgium	Macédomienne	Philippe Lafontaine	46
13	Luxembourg	Quand Je Te Rêve	Céline Carzo	38
14	Cyprus	Milas Poli	Haris Anastasiou	36
15	Netherlands	Ik Wil Alles Met Je Delen	Maywood	25
16	Sweden	Som En Vind	Edin-Ådahl	24
17	Turkey	Gözlerinin Hapsindeyim	Kayahan	21
18	Israel	Shara Barechovot	Rita	16
19	Greece	Horis Skopo	Christos Callow & Wave	11
20	Portugal	Há Sempre Alguém	Nucha	9
21	Norway	Brandenburger Tor	Ketil Stokkan	8
21	Finland	Fri?	Beat	8

The UK in Eurovision - *The Highs and Lows*

1991

POSITION	COUNTRY	SONG	ARTIST	POINTS
1	Sweden	Fångad Av En Stormvind	Carola	146
2	France	C'est Le Dernier Qui A Parlé Qui A Raison	Amina	146
3	Israel	Kan	Duo Datz	139
4	Spain	Bailar Pegados	Sergio Dalma	119
5	Switzerland	Canzone Per Te	Sandra Simó	118
6	Malta	Could It Be	Paul Giordimaina & Georgina	106
7	Italy	Comme E' Ddoce 'o Mare	Peppino di Capri	89
8	Portugal	Lusitana Paixão	Dulce	62
9	Cyprus	S.O.S.	Elena Patroclou	60
10	Ireland	Could It Be That I'm In Love	Kim Jackson	47
10	**United Kingdom**	**A Message To Your Heart**	**Samantha Janus**	**47**
12	Turkey	İki Dakika	İzel Çeliköz, Reyhan Karaca & Can Uğurluer	44
13	Greece	I Anixi	Sofia Vossou	36
14	Luxembourg	Un Baiser Volé	Sarah Bray	29
15	Iceland	Nina	Stefán & Eyfi	26
16	Belgium	Geef Het Op	Clouseau	23
17	Norway	Mrs. Thompson	Just 4 Fun	14
18	Germany	Dieser Traum Darf Niemals Sterben	Atlantis 2000	10
19	Denmark	Lige Der Hvor Hjertet Slår	Anders Frandsen	8
20	Finland	Hullu Yö	Kaija	6
21	Yugoslavia	Brazil	Baby Doll	1
22	Austria	Venedig Im Regen	Thomas Forstner	0

1992

POSITION	COUNTRY	SONG	ARTIST	POINTS
1	Ireland	Why Me	Linda Martin	155
2	**United Kingdom**	**One Step Out Of Time**	**Michael Ball**	**139**
3	Malta	Little Child	Mary Spiteri	123
4	Italy	Rapsodia	Mia Martini	111
5	Greece	Olou Tou Kosmou tin Elpida	Cleopatra	94
6	Israel	Ze Rak Sport	Dafna	85
7	Iceland	Nei Eða Já	Heart 2 Heart	80
8	France	Monté La Riviè	Kali	73
9	Netherlands	Wijs Me De Weg	Humphrey Campbell	67
10	Austria	Zusammen Geh'n	Tony Wegas	63
11	Cyprus	Teriazoume	Evridiki	57
12	Denmark	Alt Det Som Ingen Ser	Kenny & Lotte	47
13	Yugoslavia	Ljubim Te Pesmama	Extra Nena	44
14	Spain	Todo Esto Es La Música	Serafin	37
15	Switzerland	Mister Music Man	Daisy Auvray	32
16	Germany	Träume Sind Für Alle Da	Wind	27
17	Portugal	Amor D'água Fresca	Diná	26
18	Norway	Visjoner	Merethe Trøan	23
19	Turkey	Yaz Bitti	Aylin Vatankoş	17
20	Belgium	Nous On Veut Des Violons	Morgane	11
21	Luxembourg	Sou Fräi	Marion Welter and Kontinent	10
22	Sweden	I Morgon är En Annan Dag	Christer Björkman	9
23	Finland	Yamma Yamma	Pave	4

1993

POSITION	COUNTRY	SONG	ARTIST	POINTS
1	Ireland	In Your Eyes	Niamh Kavanagh	187
2	**United Kingdom**	**Better The Devil You Know**	**Sonia**	**164**
3	Switzerland	Moi, Tout Simplement	Annie Cotton	148
4	France	Mama Corsica	Patrick Fiori	121
5	Norway	Alle Mine Tankar	Silje Vige	120
6	Netherlands	Vrede	Ruth Jacott	92
7	Sweden	Eloïse	Arvingarna	89
8	Malta	This Time	William Mangion	69
9	Greece	Ellada, Hora Tou Fotos	Kaiti Garbi	64
10	Portugal	A Cidade Até Ser Dia	Anabela	60
11	Spain	Hombres	Eva Santamaria	58
12	Italy	Sole D'europa	Enrico Ruggeri	45
13	Iceland	Þá Veistu Svarið	Inga	42
14	Austria	Maria Magdalena	Tony Wegas	32
15	Croatia	Don't Ever Cry	Put	31
16	Bosnia	Sva Bol Svijeta	Fazla	27
17	Finland	Tule Luo	Katri-Helena	20
18	Germany	Viel Zu Weit	Münchener Freiheit	18
19	Cyprus	Mi Stamatas	Kyriakos Zymboulakis & Demos Van Beke	17
20	Luxembourg	Donne-moi Une Chance	Modern Times	11
21	Turkey	Esmer Yarim	Burak Aydos, Baybora & Serter Öztürk	10
22	Denmark	Under Stjernerne På Himlen	Tommy Seebach Band	9
22	Slovenia	Tih deževen dan	1X Band	9
24	Israel	Shiru	Lakahat Shiru	4
25	Belgium	Iemand Als Jij	Barbara Dex	3

1994

POSITION	COUNTRY	SONG	ARTIST	POINTS
1	Ireland	Rock 'n' Roll Kids	Paul Harrington & Charlie McGettigan	226
2	Poland	To Nie Ja!	Edyta Górniak	166
3	Germany	Wir Geben 'ne Party	MeKaDo	128
4	Hungary	Kinek Mondjam El Vétkeimet	Friderika Bayer	122
5	Malta	More Than Love	Moira Stafrace & Christopher Scicluna	97
6	Norway	Duett	Elisabeth Andreasson & Jan Werner Danielsen	76
7	France	Je Suis Un Vrai Garçon	Nina Morato	74
8	Portugal	Chamar A Música	Sara Tavares	73
9	Russia	Vechni Stranik	Youddiph	70
10	**United Kingdom**	**We Will Be Free (Lonely Symphony)**	**Frances Ruffelle**	**63**
11	Cyprus	Ime Anthropos Ke Ego	Evridiki	51
12	Iceland	Nætur	Sigga	49
13	Sweden	Stjärnorna	Marie Bergman & Roger Pontare	48
14	Greece	To Trehantiri	Costas Bigalis and the Sea Lovers	44
15	Bosnia	Ostani Kraj Mene	Alma & Dejan	39
16	Croatia	Nek'ti Bude Ljubav Sva	Tony Cetinski	27
17	Austria	Für Den Frieden Der Welt	Petra Frey	19
18	Spain	Ella No Es Ella	Alejandro Abad	17
19	Switzerland	Sto Pregando	Duilio	15
19	Slovakia	Nekonečná pieseň	Martin Ďurinda & Tublatanka	15
21	Romania	Dincolo De Nori	Dan Bittman	14
22	Finland	Bye Bye Baby	CatCat	11
23	Netherlands	Waar Is De Zon	Willeke Alberti	4
24	Estonia	Nagu Merelaine	Silvi Vrait	2
25	Lithuania	Lopšinė mylimai	Ovidijus Vyšniauskas	0

The UK in Eurovision - *The Highs and Lows*

1995

POSITION	COUNTRY	SONG	ARTIST	POINTS
1	Norway	Nocturne	Secret Garden	148
2	Spain	Vuelve Conmigo	Anabel Conde	119
3	Sweden	Se på mig	Jan Johansen	100
4	France	Il Me Donne Rendez-vous	Nathalie Santamaria	94
5	Denmark	Fra Mols Til Skagen	Aud Wilken	92
6	Croatia	Nostalgija	Magazin & Lidija	91
7	Slovenia	Prisluhni Mi	Darja Svajger	84
8	Israel	Amen	Liora	81
9	Cyprus	Sti Fotia	Alexandros Panayi	79
10	**United Kingdom**	**Love City Groove**	**Love City Groove**	**76**
10	Malta	Keep Me In Mind	Mike Spiteri	76
12	Greece	Pia Prosefhi	Elina Constantopoulou	68
13	Austria	Die Welt Dreht Sich Verkehrt	Stella Jones	67
14	Ireland	Dreamin'	Eddie Friel	44
15	Iceland	Núna	Bó Halldórsson	31
16	Turkey	Sev!	Arzu Ece	21
17	Russia	Kolybelnaya Dlya Vulkana	Philipp Kirkorov	17
18	Poland	Sama	Justyna	15
19	Bosnia	Dvadeset I Prvi Vijek	Davor Popovic	14
20	Belgium	La Voix Est Libre	Frédéric Etherlinck	8
21	Portugal	Baunilha E Chocolate	Tó Cruz	5
22	Hungary	Új név egy régi ház falán	Csaba Szigeti	3
23	Germany	Verliebt In Dich	Stone and Stone	1

1996

POSITION	COUNTRY	SONG	ARTIST	POINTS
1	Ireland	The Voice	Eimear Quinn	162
2	Norway	I Evighet	Elisabeth Andreasson	114
3	Sweden	Den Vilda	One More Time	100
4	Croatia	Sveta Ljubav	Maja Blagdan	98
5	Estonia	Kaelakee Hääl	Ivo Linna & Maarja-Liis Ilus	94
6	Portugal	O Meu Coração Não Tem Cor	Lúcia Moniz	92
7	Netherlands	De Eerste Keer	Maxine & Franklin Brown	78
8	**United Kingdom**	**Ooh... Aah... Just A Little Bit**	**Gina G**	**77**
9	Cyprus	Mono Gia Mas	Constantinos	72
10	Malta	In A Woman's Heart	Miriam Christine	68
10	Austria	Weil's Dr Guat Got	George Nußbaumer	68
12	Turkey	Beşinci Mevsim	Şebnem Paker	57
13	Iceland	Sjúbídú	Anna Mjöll	51
14	Greece	Emis Forame To Himona Anixiatika	Marianna Efstratiou	36
15	Poland	Chce Znac Swój Grzech	Kasia Kowalska	31
16	Switzerland	Mon Coeur L'aime	Cathy Leander	22
16	Belgium	Liefde Is Een Kaartspel	Lisa del Bo	22
18	Slovakia	Kým Nás Máš	Marcel Palonder	19
19	France	Diwanit Bugale	Dan Ar Braz et l'Héritage des Celtes	18
20	Spain	¡Ay, Qué Deseo!	Antonio Carbonell	17
21	Slovenia	Dan najlepših sanj	Regina	16
22	Bosnia	Za Našu Ljubav	Amila Glamocak	13
23	Finland	Niin Kaunis On Taivas	Jasmine	9

1997

POSITION	COUNTRY	SONG	ARTIST	POINTS
1	United Kingdom	Love Shine A Light	Katrina and The Waves	227
2	Ireland	Mysterious Woman	Marc Roberts	157
3	Turkey	Dinle	Şebnem Paker & Etnic	121
4	Italy	Fiumi Di Parole	Jalisse	114
5	Cyprus	Mana Mou	Chara and Andreas Konstantinou	98
6	Spain	Sin Rencor	Marcos Llunas	96
7	France	Sentiments Songes	Fanny	95
8	Estonia	Keelatud Maa	Maarja-Liis Ilus	82
9	Malta	Let Me Fly	Debbie Scerri	66
10	Slovenia	Zbudi Se	Tanja Ribič	60
11	Poland	Ale Jestem	Anna Maria Jopek	54
12	Greece	Horepse	Marianna Zorba	39
12	Hungary	Miert Kell, Hogy Elmenj?	VIP	39
14	Sweden	Bara Hon älskar Mig	Blond	36
15	Russia	Primadonna	Alla Pugachova	33
16	Denmark	Stemmen I Mit Liv	Kølig Kaj	25
17	Croatia	Probudi Me	ENI	24
18	Germany	Zeit	Bianca Shomburg	22
18	Bosnia	Goodbye	Alma Cardzic	22
20	Iceland	Minn Hinsti Dans	Paul Oscar	18
21	Austria	One Step	Bettina Soriat	12
22	Switzerland	Dentro Di Me	Barbara Berta	5
22	Netherlands	Niemand Heeft Nog Tijd	Mrs. Einstein	5
24	Norway	San Francisco	Tor Endresen	0
24	Portugal	Antes Do Adeus	Célia Lawson	0

1998

POSITION	COUNTRY	SONG	ARTIST	POINTS
1	Israel	Diva	Dana International	172
2	United Kingdom	Where Are You?	Imaani	166
3	Malta	The One That I Love	Chiara	165
4	Netherlands	Hemel En Aarde	Edsilia Rombley	150
5	Croatia	Neka Mi Ne Svane	Danijela	131
6	Belgium	Dis Oui	Mélanie Cohl	122
7	Germany	Guildo Hat Euch Lieb	Guildo Horn	86
8	Norway	Alltid Sommer	Lars A. Fredriksen	79
9	Ireland	Is Always Over Now?	Dawn	64
10	Sweden	Kärleken är	Jill Johnson	53
11	Cyprus	Genesis	Michael Hajiyanni	37
12	Portugal	Se Eu Te Pudesse Abraçar	Alma Lusa	36
12	Estonia	Mere Lapsed	Koit Toome	36
14	Turkey	Unutamazsın	Tüzmen	25
15	Finland	Aava	Edea	22
16	Spain	¿Qué Voy A Hacer Sin Ti?	Mikel Herzog	21
17	Poland	To Takie Proste	Sixteen	19
18	Slovenia	Naj Bogovi Slišijo	Vili Resnik	17
19	North Macedonia	Ne Zori, Zoro	Vlado Janevski	16
20	Greece	Mia Krifi Evaisthissia	Dionysia & Thalassa	12
21	Slovakia	Modlitba	Katarína Hasprová	8
22	Romania	Eu Cred	Malina Olinescu	6
23	Hungary	A Holnap Már Ném Lesz Szomorú	Charlie	4
24	France	Où Aller	Marie-Line	3
25	Switzerland	Lass Ihn	Gunvor	0

The UK in Eurovision - *The Highs and Lows*

1999

POSITION	COUNTRY	SONG	ARTIST	POINTS
1	Sweden	Take Me To Your Heaven	Charlotte Nilsson	163
2	Iceland	All Out Of Luck	Selma Björnsdóttir	146
3	Germany	Reise Nach Jerusalem - Kudüs'e Seyahat	Sürpriz	140
4	Croatia	Marija Magdalena	Doris Dragović	118
5	Israel	Yom Huledeth	Eden	93
6	Estonia	Diamond Of Night	Evelin Samuel & Camille	90
7	Bosnia	Putnici	Dino & Beatrice	86
8	Denmark	This Time (I Mean It)	Trine Jepsen & Michael Teschl	71
8	Netherlands	One Good Reason	Marlayne	71
10	Austria	Reflection	Bobbie Singer	65
11	Slovenia	For A Thousand Years	Darja Svajger	50
12	Belgium	Like The Wind	Venessa Chinitor	38
12	**United Kingdom**	**Say It Again**	**Precious**	**38**
14	Norway	Living My Life Without You	Stig André Van Eijk	35
15	Malta	Believe 'n Peace	Times 3	32
16	Turkey	Dön Artık	Tuba Önal & Mystık	21
17	Ireland	When You Need Me	The Mullan's	18
18	Poland	Przytul Mnie Mocno	Mietek Szczesniak	17
19	France	Je Veux Donner Ma Voix	Nayah	14
20	Lithuania	Strazdas	Aiste Smilgeviciute	13
21	Portugal	Como Tudo Começou	Rui Bandeira	12
22	Cyprus	Tha'nai Erotas	Marlain Angelidou	2
23	Spain	No Quiero Escuchar	Lydia	1

2000

POSITION	COUNTRY	SONG	ARTIST	POINTS
1	Denmark	Fly On The Wings Of Love	Olsen Brothers	195
2	Russia	Solo	Alsou	155
3	Latvia	My Star	BrainStorm	136
4	Estonia	Once In A Lifetime	Ines	98
5	Germany	Wadde Hadde Dudde Da	Stefan Raab	96
6	Ireland	Millennium Of Love	Eamonn Toal	92
7	Sweden	When Spirits Are Calling My Name	Roger Pontare	88
8	Malta	Desire	Claudette Pace	73
9	Croatia	Kada Zaspu Andeli	Goran Karan	70
10	Turkey	Yorgunum Anla	Pınar Ayhan & S.O.S. band	59
11	Norway	My Heart Goes Boom	Charmed	57
12	Iceland	Tell Me!	August & Telma	45
13	Netherlands	No Goodbyes	Linda Wagenmakers	40
14	Austria	All To You	The Rounder Girls	34
15	North Macedonia	100% Te Ljubam	XXL	29
16	**United Kingdom**	**Don't Play That Song Again**	**Nicki French**	**28**
17	Romania	The Moon	Taxi	25
18	Spain	Colgado De Un Sueño	Serafín Zubiri	18
18	Finland	A Little Bit	Nina Åström	18
20	Switzerland	La Vita Cos'è?	Jane Bogaert	14
21	Cyprus	Nomiza	Voice	8
22	Israel	Sa'me'akh	Ping Pong	7
23	France	On Aura Le Ciel	Sofia Mestari	5
24	Belgium	Envie De Vivre	Nathalie Sorce	2

2001

POSITION	COUNTRY	SONG	ARTIST	POINTS
1	Estonia	Everybody	Tanel Padar, Dave Benton & 2XL	198
2	Denmark	Never Ever Let You Go	Rollo & King	177
3	Greece	Die For You	Antique	147
4	France	Je N'ai Que Mon âme	Natasha Saint-Pier	142
5	Sweden	Listen To Your Heartbeat	Friends	100
6	Spain	Dile Que La Quiero	David Civera	76
7	Slovenia	Energy	Nuša Derenda	70
8	Germany	Wer Liebe Lebt	Michelle	66
9	Malta	Another Summer Night	Fabrizio Faniello	48
10	Croatia	Strings Of My Heart	Vanna	42
11	Turkey	Sevgiliye Son	Sedat Yüce	41
12	Russia	Lady Alpine Blue	Mumiy troll	37
13	Lithuania	You Got Style	Skamp	35
14	Bosnia & Herzegovina	Hano	Nino	29
15	**United Kingdom**	**No Dream Impossible**	**Lindsay Dracass**	**28**
16	Israel	Ein Davar	Tal Sondak	25
17	Portugal	Só Sei Ser Feliz Assim	MTM	18
18	Netherlands	Out On My Own	Michelle	16
18	Latvia	Too Much	Arnis Mednis	16
20	Poland	2 Long	Piasek	11
21	Ireland	Without Your Love	Gary O'Shaughnessy	6
22	Iceland	Angel	TwoTricky	3
22	Norway	On My Own	Haldor Lægreid	3

2002

POSITION	COUNTRY	SONG	ARTIST	POINTS
1	Latvia	I Wanna	Marie N	176
2	Malta	7th Wonder	Ira Losco	164
3	**United Kingdom**	**Come Back**	**Jessica Garlick**	**111**
3	Estonia	Runaway	Sahléne	111
5	France	Il Faut Du Temps	Sandrine François	104
6	Cyprus	Gimme	One	85
7	Spain	Europe's Living A Celebration	Rosa	81
8	Sweden	Never Let It Go	Afro-dite	72
9	Romania	Tell Me Why	Monica Anghel & Marcel Pavel	71
10	Russia	Northern Girl	Prime minister	55
11	Croatia	Everything I Want	Vesna Pisarovic	44
12	Israel	Light A Candle	Sarit Hadad	37
13	Bosnia & Herzegovina	Na Jastuku Za Dvoje	Maja	33
13	Belgium	Sister	Sergio & the Ladies	33
13	Slovenia	Samo Ljubezen	Sestre	33
16	Turkey	Leylaklar Soldu Kalbinde	Buket Dengisu & Saphire	29
17	Greece	S.A.G.A.P.O.	Michalis Rakintzis	27
18	Austria	Say A Word	Manuel Ortega	26
19	North Macedonia	Od Nas Zavisi	Karolina	25
20	Finland	Addicted To You	Laura	24
21	Germany	I Can't Live Without Music	Corinna May	17
22	Switzerland	Dans Le Jardin De Mon Âme	Francine Jordi	15
23	Lithuania	Happy You	Aivaras	12
24	Denmark	Tell Me Who You Are	Malene	7

The UK in Eurovision - *The Highs and Lows*

2003

POSITION	COUNTRY	SONG	ARTIST	POINTS
1	Turkey	Everyway That I Can	Sertab Erener	167
2	Belgium	Sanomi	Urban Trad	165
3	Russia	Ne Ver', Ne Boisia	t.A.T.u.	164
4	Norway	I'm Not Afraid To Move On	Jostein Hasselgård	123
5	Sweden	Give Me Your Love	Fame	107
6	Austria	Weil Der Mensch Zählt	Alf Poier	101
7	Poland	Keine Grenzen - Zadnych Granic	Ich Troje	90
8	Iceland	Open Your Heart	Birgitta	81
8	Spain	Dime	Beth	81
10	Romania	Don't Break My Heart	Nicola	73
11	Ireland	We've Got The World	Mickey Harte	53
11	Germany	Let's Get Happy	Lou	53
13	Netherlands	One More Night	Esther Hart	45
14	Ukraine	Hasta La Vista	Olexandr	30
15	Croatia	Više nisam tvoja	Claudia Beni	29
16	Bosnia & Herzegovina	Ne Brini	Mija Martina	27
17	Greece	Never Let You Go	Mando	25
18	France	Monts Et Merveilles	Louisa Baileche	19
19	Israel	Words For Love	Lior Narkis	17
20	Cyprus	Feeling Alive	Stelios Constantas	15
21	Estonia	Eighties Coming Back	Ruffus	14
22	Portugal	Deixa-me Sonhar	Rita Guerra	13
23	Slovenia	Nanana	Karmen	7
24	Latvia	Hello From Mars	F.L.Y.	5
25	Malta	To Dream Again	Lynn Chirchop	4
26	**United Kingdom**	**Cry Baby**	**Jemini**	**0**

2004

POSITION	COUNTRY	SONG	ARTIST	POINTS
1	Ukraine	Wild Dances	Ruslana	280
2	Serbia & Montenegro	Lane Moje	Željko Joksimović	263
3	Greece	Shake It	Sakis Rouvas	252
4	Turkey	For Real	Athena	195
5	Cyprus	Stronger Every Minute	Lisa Andreas	170
5	Sweden	It Hurts	Lena Philipsson	170
7	Albania	The Image Of You	Anjeza Shahini	106
8	Germany	Can't Wait Until Tonight	Max	93
9	Bosnia & Herzegovina	In The Disco	Deen	91
10	Spain	Para Llenarme De Ti	Ramón	87
11	Russia	Believe Me	Julia Savicheva	67
12	Malta	On again... off again	Julie & Ludwig	50
12	Croatia	You Are The Only One	Ivan Mikulic	50
14	North Macedonia	Life	Tose Proeski	47
15	France	A Chaque Pas	Jonatan Cerrada	40
16	**United Kingdom**	**Hold On To Our Love**	**James Fox**	**29**
17	Poland	Love Song	Blue Cafe	27
18	Romania	I Admit	Sanda Ladosi	18
19	Iceland	Heaven	Jónsi	16
20	Netherlands	Without You	Re-union	11
21	Austria	Du Bist	Tie Break	9
22	Belgium	1 Life	Xandee	7
22	Ireland	If My World Stopped Turning	Chris Doran	7
24	Norway	High	Knut Anders Sørum	3

2005

POSITION	COUNTRY	SONG	ARTIST	POINTS
1	Greece	My Number One	Helena Paparizou	230
2	Malta	Angel	Chiara	192
3	Romania	Let Me Try	Luminita Anghel & Sistem	158
4	Israel	Hasheket Shenish'ar	Shiri Maymon	154
5	Latvia	The War Is Not Over	Walters & Kazha	153
6	Moldova	Boonika Bate Doba	Zdob și Zdub	148
7	Serbia & Montenegro	Zauvijek Moja	No Name	137
8	Switzerland	Cool Vibes	Vanilla Ninja	128
9	Norway	In My Dreams	Wig Wam	125
9	Denmark	Talking To You	Jakob Sveistrup	125
11	Croatia	Vukovi Umiru Sami	Boris Novkovic feat. Lado members	115
12	Hungary	Forogj Világ	NOX	97
13	Turkey	Rimi Rimi Ley	Gülseren	92
14	Bosnia & Herzegovina	Call Me	Feminnem	79
15	Russia	Nobody Hurt No One	Natalia Podolskaya	57
16	Albania	Tomorrow I Go	Ledina Celo	53
17	North Macedonia	Make My Day	Martin Vucic	52
18	Cyprus	Ela Ela	Constantinos Christoforou	46
19	Sweden	Las Vegas	Martin Stenmarck	30
19	Ukraine	Razom Nas Bahato	Greenjolly	30
21	Spain	Brujería	Son de sol	28
22	**United Kingdom**	**Touch My Fire**	**Javine**	**18**
23	France	Chacun Pense à Soi	Ortal	11
24	Germany	Run & Hide	Gracia	4

2006

POSITION	COUNTRY	SONG	ARTIST	POINTS
1	Finland	Hard Rock Hallelujah	Lordi	292
2	Russia	Never Let You Go	Dima Bilan	248
3	Bosnia & Herzegovina	Lejla	Hari Mata Hari	229
4	Romania	Tornero	Mihai Traistariu	172
5	Sweden	Invincible	Carola	170
6	Lithuania	We Are The Winners	LT United	162
7	Ukraine	Show Me Your Love	Tina Karol	145
8	Armenia	Without Your Love	André	129
9	Greece	Everything	Anna Vissi	128
10	Ireland	Every Song Is A Cry For Love	Brian Kennedy	93
11	Turkey	Superstar	Sibel Tüzün	91
12	North Macedonia	Ninanajna	Elena Risteska	56
12	Croatia	Moja štikla	Severina	56
14	Norway	Alvedansen	Christine Guldbrandsen	36
14	Germany	No, No, Never	Texas Lightning	36
16	Switzerland	If We All Give A Little	Six4One	30
16	Latvia	I Hear Your Heart	Cosmos	30
18	Denmark	Twist Of Love	Sidsel Ben Semmane	26
19	**United Kingdom**	**Teenage Life**	**Daz Sampson**	**25**
20	Moldova	Loca	Arsenium & Natalia Gordienko	22
21	Spain	Bloody Mary	Las Ketchup	18
22	France	Il était Temps	Virginie Pouchin	5
23	Israel	Ze Hazman	Eddie Butler	4
24	Malta	I Do	Fabrizio Faniello	1

The UK in Eurovision - *The Highs and Lows*

2007

POSITION	COUNTRY	SONG	ARTIST	POINTS
1	Serbia	Molitva	Marija Šerifović	268
2	Ukraine	Dancing Lasha Tumbai	Verka Serduchka	235
3	Russia	Song # 1	Serebro	207
4	Turkey	Shake It Up Shekerim	Kenan Dogulu	163
5	Bulgaria	Water	Elitsa Todorova & Stoyan Yankulov	157
6	Belarus	Work Your Magic	Dmitry Koldun	145
7	Greece	Yassou Maria	Sarbel	139
8	Armenia	Anytime You Need	Hayko	138
9	Hungary	Unsubstantial Blues	Magdi Rúzsa	128
10	Moldova	Fight	Natalia Barbu	109
11	Bosnia & Herzegovina	Rijeka Bez Imena	Marija Sestic	106
12	Georgia	Visionary Dream	Sopho	97
13	Romania	Liubi, Liubi, I Love You	Todomondo	84
14	North Macedonia	Mojot Svet	Karolina	73
15	Slovenia	Cvet Z Juga	Alenka Gotar	66
16	Latvia	Questa Notte	Bonaparti.lv	54
17	Finland	Leave Me Alone	Hanna Pakarinen	53
18	Sweden	The Worrying Kind	The Ark	51
19	Germany	Frauen Regieren Die Welt	Roger Cicero	49
20	Spain	I Love You Mi Vida	NASH	43
21	Lithuania	Love Or Leave	4Fun	28
22	France	L'amour à La Française	Les Fatals Picards	19
22	**United Kingdom**	**Flying The Flag (for You)**	**Scooch**	**19**
24	Ireland	They Can't Stop The Spring	Dervish	5

2008

POSITION	COUNTRY	SONG	ARTIST	POINTS
1	Russia	Believe	Dima Bilan	272
2	Ukraine	Shady Lady	Ani Lorak	230
3	Greece	Secret Combination	Kalomira	218
4	Armenia	Qele, Qele	Sirusho	199
5	Norway	Hold On Be Strong	Maria	182
6	Serbia	Oro	Jelena Tomašević feat. Bora Dugic	160
7	Turkey	Deli	Mor ve Ötesi	138
8	Azerbaijan	Day After Day	Elnur & Samir	132
9	Israel	The Fire In Your Eyes	Boaz	124
10	Bosnia & Herzegovina	Pokušaj	Laka	110
11	Georgia	Peace Will Come	Diana Gurtskaya	83
12	Latvia	Wolves Of The Sea	Pirates Of The Sea	83
13	Portugal	Senhora Do Mar (Negras Águas)	Vânia Fernandes	69
14	Iceland	This Is My Life	Euroband	64
15	Denmark	All Night Long	Simon Mathew	60
16	Spain	Baila El Chiki Chiki	Rodolfo Chikilicuatre	55
17	Albania	Zemrën E Lamë Peng	Olta Boka	55
18	Sweden	Hero	Charlotte Perrelli	47
19	France	Divine	Sébastien Tellier	47
20	Romania	Pe-o Margine De Lume	Nico & Vlad	45
21	Croatia	Romanca	Kraljevi Ulice & 75 Cents	44
22	Finland	Missä Miehet Ratsastaa	Teräsbetoni	35
23	Germany	Disappear	No Angels	14
24	Poland	For Life	Isis Gee	14
25	**United Kingdom**	**Even If**	**Andy Abraham**	**14**

2009

POSITION	COUNTRY	SONG	ARTIST	POINTS
1	Norway	Fairytale	Alexander Rybak	387
2	Iceland	Is It True?	Yohanna	218
3	Azerbaijan	Always	AySel & Arash	207
4	Turkey	Düm Tek Tek	Hadise	177
5	**United Kingdom**	**It's My Time**	**Jade Ewen**	**173**
6	Estonia	Rändajad	Urban Symphony	129
7	Greece	This Is Our Night	Sakis Rouvas	120
8	France	Et S'il Fallait Le Faire	Patricia Kaas	107
9	Bosnia & Herzegovina	Bistra Voda	Regina	106
10	Armenia	Jan Jan	Inga & Anush	92
11	Russia	Mamo	Anastasia Prikhodko	91
12	Ukraine	Be my Valentine! (Anti-crisis Girl)	Svetlana Loboda	76
13	Denmark	Believe Again	Brinck	74
14	Moldova	Hora Din Moldova	Nelly Ciobanu	69
15	Portugal	Todas As Ruas Do Amor	Flor-de-lis	57
16	Israel	There Must Be Another Way	Noa & Mira Awad	53
17	Albania	Carry Me In Your Dreams	Kejsi Tola	48
18	Croatia	Lijepa Tena	Igor Cukrov feat. Andrea	45
19	Romania	The Balkan Girls	Elena	40
20	Germany	Miss Kiss Kiss Bang	Alex Swings Oscar Sings!	35
21	Sweden	La Voix	Malena Ernman	33
22	Malta	What If We	Chiara	31
23	Lithuania	Love	Sasha Son	23
24	Spain	La Noche Es Para Mí	Soraya	23

2010

POSITION	COUNTRY	SONG	ARTIST	POINTS
1	Germany	Satellite	Lena	246
2	Turkey	We Could Be The Same	maNga	170
3	Romania	Playing With Fire	Paula Seling & Ovi	162
4	Denmark	In A Moment Like This	Chanée & N'evergreen	149
5	Azerbaijan	Drip Drop	Safura	145
6	Belgium	Me And My Guitar	Tom Dice	143
7	Armenia	Apricot Stone	Eva Rivas	141
8	Greece	OPA	Giorgos Alkaios & Friends	140
9	Georgia	Shine	Sofia Nizharadze	136
10	Ukraine	Sweet People	Alyosha	108
11	Russia	Lost And Forgotten	Peter Nalitch & Friends	90
12	France	Allez Ola Olé	Jessy Matador	82
13	Serbia	Ovo Je Balkan	Milan Stanković	72
14	Israel	Milim	Harel Skaat	71
15	Spain	Algo Pequeñito	Daniel Diges	68
16	Albania	It's All About You	Juliana Pasha	62
17	Bosnia & Herzegovina	Thunder and Lightning	Vukašin Brajić	51
18	Portugal	Há Dias Assim	Filipa Azevedo	43
19	Iceland	Je Ne Sais Quoi	Hera Björk	41
20	Norway	My Heart Is Yours	Didrik Solli-Tangen	35
21	Cyprus	Life Looks Better In Spring	Jon Lilygreen & The Islanders	27
22	Moldova	Run Away	Sunstroke Project & Olia Tira	27
23	Ireland	It's For You	Niamh Kavanagh	25
24	Belarus	Butterflies	3+2	18
25	**United Kingdom**	**That Sounds Good To Me**	**Josh**	**10**

The UK in Eurovision - *The Highs and Lows*

2011

POSITION	COUNTRY	SONG	ARTIST	POINTS
1	Azerbaijan	Running Scared	Ell/Nikki	221
2	Italy	Madness Of Love	Raphael Gualazzi	189
3	Sweden	Popular	Eric Saade	185
4	Ukraine	Angel	Mika Newton	159
5	Denmark	New Tomorrow	A Friend In London	134
6	Bosnia & Herzegovina	Love In Rewind	Dino Merlin	125
7	Greece	Watch My Dance	Loucas Yiorkas feat. Stereo Mike	120
8	Ireland	Lipstick	Jedward	119
9	Georgia	One More Day	Eldrine	110
10	Germany	Taken By A Stranger	Lena	107
11	**United Kingdom**	**I Can**	**Blue**	**100**
12	Moldova	So Lucky	Zdob și Zdub	97
13	Slovenia	No One	Maja Keuc	96
14	Serbia	Čaroban	Nina	85
15	France	Sognu	Amaury Vassili	82
16	Russia	Get You	Alexej Vorobjov	77
17	Romania	Change	Hotel FM	77
18	Austria	The Secret Is Love	Nadine Beiler	64
19	Lithuania	C'est Ma Vie	Evelina Sašenko	63
20	Iceland	Coming Home	Sjonni's Friends	61
21	Finland	Da Da Dam	Paradise Oskar	57
22	Hungary	What About My Dreams?	Kati Wolf	53
23	Spain	Que Me Quiten Lo Bailao	Lucía Pérez	50
24	Estonia	Rockefeller Street	Getter Jaani	44
25	Switzerland	In Love For A While	Anna Rossinelli	19

2012

POSITION	COUNTRY	SONG	ARTIST	POINTS
1	Sweden	Euphoria	Loreen	372
2	Russia	Party For Everybody	Buranovskiye Babushki	259
3	Serbia	Nije Ljubav Stvar	Željko Joksimović	214
4	Azerbaijan	When The Music Dies	Sabina Babayeva	150
5	Albania	Suus	Rona Nishliu	146
6	Estonia	Kuula	Ott Lepland	120
7	Turkey	Love Me Back	Can Bonomo	112
8	Germany	Standing Still	Roman Lob	110
9	Italy	L'Amore È Femmina (Out Of Love)	Nina Zilli	101
10	Spain	Quédate Conmigo	Pastora Soler	97
11	Moldova	Lăutar	Pasha Parfeny	81
12	Romania	Zaleilah	Mandinga	71
13	North Macedonia	Crno I Belo	Kaliopi	71
14	Lithuania	Love Is Blind	Donny Montell	70
15	Ukraine	Be My Guest	Gaitana	65
16	Cyprus	La La Love	Ivi Adamou	65
17	Greece	Aphrodisiac	Eleftheria Eleftheriou	64
18	Bosnia & Herzegovina	Korake Ti Znam	Maya Sar	55
19	Ireland	Waterline	Jedward	46
20	Iceland	Never Forget	Greta Salóme & Jónsi	46
21	Malta	This Is The Night	Kurt Calleja	41
22	France	Echo (You And I)	Anggun	21
23	Denmark	Should've Known Better	Soluna Samay	21
24	Hungary	Sound Of Our Hearts	Compact Disco	19
25	**United Kingdom**	**Love Will Set You Free**	**Engelbert Humperdinck**	**12**
26	Norway	Stay	Tooji	7

2013

POSITION	COUNTRY	SONG	ARTIST	POINTS
1	Denmark	Only Teardrops	Emmelie de Forest	281
2	Azerbaijan	Hold Me	Farid Mammadov	234
3	Ukraine	Gravity	Zlata Ognevich	214
4	Norway	I Feed You My Love	Margaret Berger	191
5	Russia	What If	Dina Garipova	174
6	Greece	Alcohol Is Free	Koza Mostra feat. Agathon Iakovidis	152
7	Italy	L'Essenziale	Marco Mengoni	126
8	Malta	Tomorrow	Gianluca	120
9	Netherlands	Birds	Anouk	114
10	Hungary	Kedvesem	ByeAlex	84
11	Moldova	O Mie	Aliona Moon	71
12	Belgium	Love Kills	Roberto Bellarosa	71
13	Romania	It's My Life	Cezar	65
14	Sweden	You	Robin Stjernberg	62
15	Georgia	Waterfall	Nodi Tatishvili & Sophie Gelovani	50
16	Belarus	Solayoh	Alyona Lanskaya	48
17	Iceland	Ég Á Líf	Eythor Ingi	47
18	Armenia	Lonely Planet	Dorians	41
19	**United Kingdom**	**Believe In Me**	**Bonnie Tyler**	**23**
20	Estonia	Et Uus Saaks Alguse	Birgit	19
21	Germany	Glorious	Cascada	18
22	Lithuania	Something	Andrius Pojavis	17
23	France	L'enfer Et Moi	Amandine Bourgeois	14
24	Finland	Marry Me	Krista Siegfrids	13
25	Spain	Contigo Hasta El Final	ESDM	8
26	Ireland	Only Love Survives	Ryan Dolan	5

2014

POSITION	COUNTRY	SONG	ARTIST	POINTS
1	Austria	Rise Like a Phoenix	Conchita Wurst	290
2	Netherlands	Calm After The Storm	The Common Linnets	238
3	Sweden	Undo	Sanna Nielsen	218
4	Armenia	Not Alone	Aram MP3	174
5	Hungary	Running	András Kállay-Saunders	143
6	Ukraine	Tick - Tock	Mariya Yaremchuk	113
7	Russia	Shine	Tolmachevy Sisters	89
8	Norway	Silent Storm	Carl Espen	88
9	Denmark	Cliche Love Song	Basim	74
10	Spain	Dancing in the rain	Ruth Lorenzo	74
11	Finland	Something Better	Softengine	72
12	Romania	Miracle	Paula Seling & OVI	72
13	Switzerland	Hunter Of Stars	Sebalter	64
14	Poland	My Słowianie - We Are Slavic	Donatan & Cleo	62
15	Iceland	No Prejudice	Pollapönk	58
16	Belarus	Cheesecake	Teo	43
17	**United Kingdom**	**Children of the Universe**	**Molly**	**40**
18	Germany	Is It Right	Elaiza	39
19	Montenegro	Moj Svijet	Sergej Ćetković	37
20	Greece	Rise Up	Freaky Fortune feat. RiskyKidd	35
21	Italy	La Mia Città	Emma	33
22	Azerbaijan	Start A Fire	Dilara Kazimova	33
23	Malta	Coming Home	Firelight	32
24	San	Maybe (Forse)	Valentina Monetta	14
25	Slovenia	Round and Round	Tinkara Kovač	9
26	France	Moustache	TWIN TWIN	2

The UK in Eurovision - *The Highs and Lows*

2015

POSITION	COUNTRY	SONG	ARTIST	POINTS
1	Sweden	Heroes	Måns Zelmerlöw	365
2	Russia	A Million Voices	Polina Gagarina	303
3	Italy	Grande Amore	Il Volo	292
4	Belgium	Rhythm Inside	Loïc Nottet	217
5	Australia	Tonight Again	Guy Sebastian	196
6	Latvia	Love Injected	Aminata Savadogo	186
7	Estonia	Goodbye to Yesterday	Elina Born & Stig Rästa	106
8	Norway	A Monster Like Me	Mørland & Debrah Scarlett	102
9	Israel	Golden Boy	Nadav Guedj	97
10	Serbia	Beauty Never Lies	Bojana Stamenov	53
11	Georgia	Warrior	Nina Sublatti	51
12	Azerbaijan	Hour Of The Wolf	Elnur Hüseynov	49
13	Montenegro	Adio	Knez	44
14	Slovenia	Here for You	Maraaya	39
15	Romania	De La Capăt / All Over Again	Voltaj	35
16	Armenia	Face The Shadow	Genealogy	34
17	Albania	I'm Alive	Elhaida Dani	34
18	Lithuania	This Time	Monika & Vaidas	30
19	Greece	One Last Breath	Maria Elena Kyriakou	23
20	Hungary	Wars For Nothing	Boggie	19
21	Spain	Amanecer	Edurne	15
22	Cyprus	One Thing I Should Have Done	John Karayiannis	11
23	Poland	In The Name Of Love	Monika Kuszyńska	10
24	**United Kingdom**	**Still in Love with You**	**Electro Velvet**	**5**
25	France	N'oubliez pas	Lisa Angell	4
26	Austria	I Am Yours	The Makemakes	0
27	Germany	Black Smoke	Ann Sophie	0

2016

POSITION	COUNTRY	SONG	ARTIST	POINTS
1	Ukraine	1944	Jamala	534
2	Australia	Sound of Silence	Dami Im	511
3	Russia	You Are the Only One	Sergey Lazarev	491
4	Bulgaria	If Love Was a Crime	Poli Genova	307
5	Sweden	If I Were Sorry	Frans	261
6	France	J'ai Cherché	Amir	257
7	Armenia	LoveWave	Iveta Mukuchyan	249
8	Poland	Color of Your Life	Michał Szpak	229
9	Lithuania	I've Been Waiting for This Night	Donny Montell	200
10	Belgium	What's the Pressure	Laura Tesoro	181
11	Netherlands	Slow Down	Douwe Bob	153
12	Malta	Walk on Water	Ira Losco	153
13	Austria	Loin d'ici	Zoë	151
14	Israel	Made of Stars	Hovi Star	135
15	Latvia	Heartbeat	Justs	132
16	Italy	No Degree of Separation	Francesca Michielin	124
17	Azerbaijan	Miracle	Samra	117
18	Serbia	Goodbye (Shelter)	Sanja Vučić ZAA	115
19	Hungary	Pioneer	Freddie	108
20	Georgia	Midnight Gold	Nika Kocharov & Young Georgian Lolitaz	104
21	Cyprus	Alter Ego	Minus One	96
22	Spain	Say Yay!	Barei	77
23	Croatia	Lighthouse	Nina Kraljić	73
24	**United Kingdom**	**You're Not Alone**	**Joe & Jake**	**62**
25	Czechia	I Stand	Gabriela Gunčíková	41
26	Germany	Ghost	Jamie-Lee Kriewitz	11

2017

POSITION	COUNTRY	SONG	ARTIST	POINTS
1	Portugal	Amar Pelos Dois	Salvador Sobral	758
2	Bulgaria	Beautiful Mess	Kristian Kostov	615
3	Moldova	Hey Mamma	Sunstroke Project	374
4	Belgium	City Lights	Blanche	363
5	Sweden	I Can't Go On	Robin Bengtsson	344
6	Italy	Occidentali's Karma	Francesco Gabbani	334
7	Romania	Yodel It!	Ilinca feat. Alex Florea	282
8	Hungary	Origo	Joci Pápai	200
9	Australia	Don't Come Easy	Isaiah	173
10	Norway	Grab the Moment	Jowst	158
11	Netherlands	Lights And Shadows	OG3NE	150
12	France	Requiem	Alma	135
13	Croatia	My Friend	Jacques Houdek	128
14	Azerbaijan	Skeletons	Dihaj	120
15	**United Kingdom**	**Never Give Up on You**	**Lucie Jones**	**111**
16	Austria	Running On Air	Nathan Trent	93
17	Belarus	Historyja majho žyccia	Naviband	83
18	Armenia	Fly With Me	Artsvik	79
19	Greece	This is Love	Demy	77
20	Denmark	Where I Am	Anja	77
21	Cyprus	Gravity	Hovig	68
22	Poland	Flashlight	Kasia Moś	64
23	Israel	I Feel Alive	Imri Ziv	39
24	Ukraine	Time	O.Torvald	36
25	Germany	Perfect Life	Levina	6
26	Spain	Do It for Your Lover	Manel Navarro	5

2018

POSITION	COUNTRY	SONG	ARTIST	POINTS
1	Israel	Toy	Netta	529
2	Cyprus	Fuego	Eleni Foureira	436
3	Austria	Nobody But You	Cesár Sampson	342
4	Germany	You Let Me Walk Alone	Michael Schulte	340
5	Italy	Non Mi Avete Fatto Niente	Ermal Meta & Fabrizio Moro	308
6	Czechia	Lie To Me	Mikolas Josef	281
7	Sweden	Dance You Off	Benjamin Ingrosso	274
8	Estonia	La Forza	Elina Nechayeva	245
9	Denmark	Higher Ground	Rasmussen	226
10	Moldova	My Lucky Day	DoReDos	209
11	Albania	Mall	Eugent Bushpepa	184
12	Lithuania	When We're Old	Ieva Zasimauskaitė	181
13	France	Mercy	Madame Monsieur	173
14	Bulgaria	Bones	Equinox	166
15	Norway	That's How You Write a Song	Alexander Rybak	144
16	Ireland	Together	Ryan O'Shaughnessy	136
17	Ukraine	Under the Ladder	Mélovin	130
18	Netherlands	Outlaw In 'Em	Waylon	121
19	Serbia	Nova Deca	Sanja Ilić & Balkanika	113
20	Australia	We Got Love	Jessica Mauboy	99
21	Hungary	Viszlát Nyár	AWS	93
22	Slovenia	Hvala, ne!	Lea Sirk	64
23	Spain	Tu Canción	Amaia & Alfred	61
24	**United Kingdom**	**Storm**	**SuRie**	**48**
25	Finland	Monsters	Saara Aalto	46
26	Portugal	O Jardim	Cláudia Pascoal	39

2019

POSITION	COUNTRY	SONG	ARTIST	POINTS
1	Netherlands	Arcade	Duncan Laurence	498
2	Italy	Soldi	Mahmood	472
3	Russia	Scream	Sergey Lazarev	370
4	Switzerland	She Got Me	Luca Hänni	364
5	Sweden	Too Late for Love	John Lundvik	334
6	Norway	Spirit in the Sky	KEiiNO	331
7	North Macedonia	Proud	Tamara Todevska	305
8	Azerbaijan	Truth	Chingiz	302
9	Australia	Zero Gravity	Kate Miller-Heidke	284
10	Iceland	Hatrið mun sigra	Hatari	232
11	Czechia	Friend of a Friend	Lake Malawi	157
12	Denmark	Love Is Forever	Leonora	120
13	Cyprus	Replay	Tamta	109
14	Malta	Chameleon	Michela	107
15	Slovenia	Sebi	Zala Kralj & Gašper Šantl	105
16	France	Roi	Bilal Hassani	105
17	Albania	Ktheju Tokës	Jonida Maliqi	90
18	Serbia	Kruna	Nevena Božović	89
19	San	Say Na Na Na	Serhat	77
20	Estonia	Storm	Victor Crone	76
21	Greece	Better Love	Katerine Duska	74
22	Spain	La Venda	Miki	54
23	Israel	Home	Kobi Marimi	35
24	Belarus	Like It	Zena	31
25	Germany	Sister	Sisters	24
26	**United Kingdom**	**Bigger Than Us**	**Michael Rice**	11

2020
Covid Pandemic

2021

POSITION	COUNTRY	SONG	ARTIST	POINTS
1	Italy	Zitti e buoni	Måneskin	524
2	France	Voilà	Barbara Pravi	499
3	Switzerland	Tout l'univers	Gjon's Tears	432
4	Iceland	10 Years	Daði & Gagnamagnið	378
5	Ukraine	Shum	Go_A	364
6	Finland	Dark Side	Blind Channel	301
7	Malta	Je Me Casse	Destiny	255
8	Lithuania	Discoteque	The Roop	220
9	Russia	Russian Woman	Manizha	204
10	Greece	Last Dance	Stefania	170
11	Bulgaria	Growing Up Is Getting Old	Victoria	170
12	Portugal	Love Is On My Side	The Black Mamba	153
13	Moldova	Sugar	Natalia Gordienko	115
14	Sweden	Voices	Tusse	109
15	Serbia	Loco Loco	Hurricane	102
16	Cyprus	El Diablo	Elena Tsagrinou	94
17	Israel	Set Me Free	Eden Alene	93
18	Norway	Fallen Angel	TIX	75
19	Belgium	The Wrong Place	Hooverphonic	74
20	Azerbaijan	Mata Hari	Efendi	65
21	Albania	Karma	Anxhela Peristeri	57
22	San	Adrenalina	Senhit feat. Flo Rida	50
23	Netherlands	Birth Of A New Age	Jeangu Macrooy	11
24	Spain	Voy A Quedarme	Blas Cantó	6
25	Germany	I Don't Feel Hate	Jendrik	3
26	**United Kingdom**	**Embers**	**James Newman**	**0**

2022

POSITION	COUNTRY	SONG	ARTIST	POINTS
1	Ukraine	Stefania	Kalush Orchestra	631
2	**United Kingdom**	**Space Man**	**Sam Ryder**	**466**
3	Spain	SloMo	Chanel	459
4	Sweden	Hold Me Closer	Cornelia Jakobs	438
5	Serbia	In Corpore Sano	Konstrakta	312
6	Italy	Brividi	Mahmood & Blanco	268
7	Moldova	Trenulețul	Zdob și Zdub & Advahov Brothers	253
8	Greece	Die Together	Amanda Georgiadi Tenfjord	215
9	Portugal	Saudade, saudade	Maro	207
10	Norway	Give That Wolf a Banana	Subwoolfer	182
11	Netherlands	De Diepte	S10	171
12	Poland	River	Ochman	151
13	Estonia	Hope	Stefan	141
14	Lithuania	Sentimentai	Monika Liu	128
15	Australia	Not The Same	Sheldon Riley	125
16	Azerbaijan	Fade To Black	Nadir Rustamli	106
17	Switzerland	Boys Do Cry	Marius Bear	78
18	Romania	Llámame	WRS	65
19	Belgium	Miss You	Jérémie Makiese	64
20	Armenia	Snap	Rosa Linn	61
21	Finland	Jezebel	The Rasmus	38
22	Czechia	Lights Off	We Are Domi	38
23	Iceland	Með hækkandi sól	Systur	20
24	France	Fulenn	Alvan & Ahez	17
25	Germany	Rockstars	Malik Harris	6

References

Newspapers.com
Daily Mail
Daily Express
The Independent
The Guardian
The Sunday Telegraph
BBC
Many Regional Newspapers were used for local facts
Eurovisionworld.com
Wikipedia
The Complete and Independent Guide to the Eurovision Song Contest - Simon Barclay

Acknowledgements

A big shout out to Jerry and Gary at Wymer Publishing for having faith in me and publishing this book, and special thanks for Jerry with his spreadsheet skills and helping out with the tables at the back of the book.
Also a special thanks to my long suffering wife and kids for putting up with me.
One other thing if you are reading this, you have probably bought my book so a very big thankyou for that. Hope you enjoy it.